PERFUME

OF THE

DESERT

✦

PERFUME

OF THE

DESERT

INSPIRATIONS FROM

SUFI WISDOM

ANDREW HARVEY

AND

ERYK HANUT

A publication supported by
THE KERN FOUNDATION

Quest Books
Theosophical Publishing House
Wheaton, Illinois ◆ Chennai (Madras), India

The Theosophical Publishing House
P.O. Box 270
Wheaton, IL 60189-0270

A publication of the Theosophical Publishing House, a department
of the Theosophical Society in America

Cover and book design by Beth Hansen-Winter

Library of Congress Cataloging-in-Publication Data

Harvey, Andrew.
    Perfume of the desert: inspirations from Sufi wisdom / Andrew
Harvey and Eryk Hanut. — 1st Quest ed.
    p.   cm.
    ISBN 0-8356-0767-4
    1. Sufism.   2. Sufi literature.   3. Sufism in literature.
    I. Harvey, Andrew.   II. Title.
BP189.H337   1999
297.4 — dc21   98-44314
                                                  CIP

4   3   2   1   ❋   99   00   01   02   03   04   05

Printed in the United States of America

For Karen Kellejian,

kindest of companions on the Path,
with our love and gratitude always.

A.H. *and* E.H.

CONTENTS

Introduction

BY ANDREW HARVEY

In my early twenties, I read a Sufi story in a book on Lawrence of Arabia that has haunted me ever since. This is how I remember it: A group of wild young Bedouins were riding in the desert with their chief, who was a religious man as well as a great leader. They came in the course of their wanderings to a vast ruined palace. The young men rode through the deserted rooms, breaking off bits of the plaster and brick to smell what had gone into their making. One cried out, "In this clay are mixed the oils of rose and orange-blossom." Another exclaimed, "In this dirt I smell jasmine! How beautiful!"

The chief stood apart and said nothing. When the young men had ridden through all of the rooms, savoring the various fragrances that could still be smelled in the clay of the ruined palace, they asked the chief, "And what is your favorite perfume?" He smiled and leaned as far as he could out of one of the palace windows into the empty desert wind. He reached out his hands and cupped them. Then he held out his cupped hands to the young men and said, "Smell this! The best perfume of all is the perfume of the desert, for it smells of nothing."

A decade later I was sitting in Paris with an old Sufi friend —
a great translator, scholar, and seeker with whom I was working
on translations of Rumi. I told her the story and asked her what it
meant for her. She did not speak for a long time and then she said:

*For me, whenever I think of the Sufis and of Sufism, I think of
the desert. I think of the desert's wildness, its gorgeous and terrible loneliness, its silence, its purity. I think of how in the desert
you feel at once annihilated yet totally alive and present in all
things around you and above you, as if you had become at once
the sands stretching from horizon to horizon and the sky, so vast
and empty and still. And I think too of what is written in the
Koran, "All is perishable except the Face of God." The desert is
the Face of God, the final mirror in which human beings see their
nothingness and their absolute splendor-in-Him. The Sufis are
those who spend their lives looking into the mirror of the desert,
and in holding up the purity, glory, and rigor of the desert to their
lives. And in the greatest Sufi philosophers and poets you smell
what the chief in the story calls the "best perfume of all" — the
perfume of the desert, the fragrance of the void, the ecstatic sweet
inebriating perfume of the Presence that is at once Everything
and Nothing.*

I was moved by what she said but I wanted her to speak
about the story itself. So I asked her to tell me what the story had
told her. *"To me it is clear,"* she said.

Perhaps being in my early eighties helps it be so clear. The ruined palace is the world and all its games and desires and projects; each of them is made from some "aromatic" desire that leaves a lingering trace. A line from T.S. Eliot's Four Quartets *comes back to me: "Ash on an old man's sleeve / Is all the ash the burnt roses leave." All the world's joys, however beautiful, are passing and cannot be kept long. The one eternal perfume is the one that smells of the Nothing of God; it is this "perfume"—this gnosis, this bliss and ecstasy—that all mystics seek to "smell" because they know it makes them drunk on the Beloved and lures them on to realize their identity with Him.*

She paused and looked at her old arthritic hands, smiling wryly. *"And once you have smelled that perfume, your life is ruined because nothing else will ever be as fragrant and your whole being becomes longing."*

And then she told me a Sufi story. *"You have told me a story that moves you; now I will tell you one I love. I think they are linked and that if you listen to your story and my story together, you can hear almost the whole music of Sufism in them.*

"I heard this story on my first visit to Konya where Rumi lived and when I heard it something changed in my heart forever."

There was an emperor who had a slave he loved passionately and who, he believed, loved him with his whole self. But the Emperor wanted to be certain. So he filled ten rooms with heaps of every kind of treasure imaginable — rubies and emeralds, strands of large black pearls, chests full of the richest cloths and rarest, most marvelously illuminated manuscripts, large leather wallets with deeds in them to houses and country estates. When the rooms were full of this treasure, and the walls of the rooms seemed to glow and shine in the radiance of so much glory, the Emperor summoned everyone in his court and all his servants and slaves and said, "Today I am releasing you all from my service. You are at perfect liberty to take anything you want from any of the rooms before you." You can well imagine what pandemonium broke out! Even the Chief Vizier, normally a rather austere kind of man, started to dance a jig and to cram under his arms as many jewels and house deeds as he could find.

She paused and gazed out of the window and the noise from the Parisian street below seemed to subside.

"But the slave whom the Emperor loved so did not move," she said, her voice trembling slightly.

He stayed standing where he was, silently, his face gazing at the Emperor until all the treasure was gone and only he and the Emperor were left in a desert of empty rooms. The Emperor said quietly, "And you, who have stayed and not sought for anything for yourself, what is it you want? You can have anything you want in any of the worlds I own." The slave still said nothing, and then the Emperor almost shouted, "What is it that you want?

I order you to tell me!" And the slave said, "I want you." He repeated very slowly, "I want you. I want you." That was what he, the real Sufi, wanted—not the palace, or power, or any of the jewels and other gifts of the Emperor—but the Emperor himself.

She leaned back into the shadow of her chair and recited a poem by Rumi:

You are a sea of gnosis hidden in a drop of dew.
You are a whole universe hidden in a sack of blood.
What are all these worlds, pleasures, and joys
That you keep grasping at them to make you alive?

A profound silence fell between us. Then she said,

To smell the "perfume of the desert" you have to learn to love like that slave loved his Emperor. People ask me all the time what I think Sufism is. Sometimes, when I'm lazy, I tell them it is the "esoteric side of Islam" or trot out the quotation of some Sufi sage or philosopher. But when I am feeling reckless I just say "Sufism is the ancient wisdom of the heart. It predates Islam as Eternity predates time. It has always been there from the beginning of human adoration of God. Sufism is the ancient wisdom of the heart and the science of love born from that wisdom, a science as precise but far more beneficial than the external sciences, perfected over centuries of brave exploration of the Desert of the Ab-

*solute." Did you know that the word for mystic path in Sufism —
tariqah — means the path in the desert that the Bedouin takes to
travel from oasis to oasis? Obviously such a path is not clearly
marked like a highway and isn't even a visible road. But it is
there to those who know. To find your way in the trackless desert
you need to know the area intimately. Sufis are those who know
the area intimately.*

In the decade since that conversation, Sufism has come to
attract ever-growing numbers of seekers and to enjoy an extraor-
dinary renaissance throughout the Western world.

The main reason for this, I think, is that the Sufi approach to
reality and to the quest for God is extremely passionate. The passion that the Sufi mystic prays for is one that embraces all of
reality as a manifestation of the Divine and longs to burn itself
out in the fire of love. Such a passion devours everything, is a
furnace into which all other passions, desires, and agendas are
quickly incinerated. Such a passion also costs everything, for the
whole being and all its powers have to be strenuously devoted to
it at all moments and in all circumstances to keep it alive and
aflame. Rumi speaks in his *Odes* that this passion is a "howling
storm in which all the houses of the false self are flattened forever."

In a passionless and psychologically devastated time like ours,
the witness of the great Sufi saints and philosophers to this highest, noblest, and most devastating of all human passions — that of

the soul for the Beloved — has an enormous force for awakening. Our modern addictions to reason and the games of irony and control have drained our psyches and souls of the heart-blood that keeps life abundant and miraculous; the Sufi lovers pump back that blood into us, fill us in fact with their blood, that long adoration and gnosis has turned into the purest — and most inebriating — mystic wine. The passion of the Sufi witnesses to the always-shattering glory of the Beloved and to the splendor of the journey towards Him which restores us to the greatness of our real life, its vast capacity for suffering and joy, the measureless growth of spirit that we are capable of if we let ourselves be possessed and devoured by Divine Love.

All authentic passion has great rigor, and true Sufi mysticism is nothing if not rigorous. The way of love demands from all who take it a terrible sincerity of being and a commitment to die again and again into the Nothing of the Divine. The Sufi mystical philosophers and poets face unsparingly all the ordeals and devastations of authentic transformation: their work has the "sear-marks" as well as the perfume of the desert. As my friend said that afternoon in Paris, "They know the area intimately," and we know that they know, because they speak to us with the broken-hearted authority of real lovers. They tell us in the most naked, arresting, and human way, exactly what Love demands of us and what its multiple deaths feel like. Because they have so extreme and gorgeous a vision and knowledge of Love's glory, they never pretend that it is not worth all the horrors and ordeals of the journey towards it, and they never sell short the dangers that every soul must face on its voyage to the Absolute. They are reliable guides to the *tariqah* that crosses the desert of the Absolute and take us from oasis to oasis of gnosis and revelation with an effortlessness — and above all, a purity of address — which will astonish and hearten all those who turn to them for help.

The greatest Sufis speak to us with a voice that is as practical as it is passionate, and this mixture of passion and practicality is one of the peculiar greatnesses of Sufism and another deep reason for its modern appeal. There is, of course, a strong ascetic tradition within Sufism: many of the greatest Sufi saints — particularly in the early period of the development of Sufism — were, like Rabia, seekers who abandoned the world to concentrate wholly on God; but the majority of the greatest Sufis have been men and women who lived in the world and who used its frictions, terrors, and tensions as ways of deepening their practice of Presence and as constant tests of their stability and sincerity. The highest ideals in Sufism, as in Christianity, are ones not of flight from the world but of living with divine peace, truth, and sobriety in it, and in a state of servanthood towards all beings and creatures. The Sufis are extremely wise guides to that integration that must happen on every level of our being if we are not only to glimpse the Absolute but also to live it at the heart of the inferno of ordinary life with all its distractions and worries. The Sufi tradition offers us not only a vast and complex witness to the ecstasy and passion of the path of love, but also a practical guide on how to integrate ecstasy and passion with the demands of everyday life. This fusion of drunkenness and sobriety, the highest and wildest kinds of gnosis with the most considered understanding of how to infuse dailiness with Divine Truth, is what makes Sufism one of the world's indispensable mystical traditions, one that seekers of all kinds have everything to learn from, especially in an era as deranged as ours.

In the hope of awakening the sacred heart in all of us and infusing its passion into all the choices of life, I have created this anthology. I have chosen to include only those poems, stories, or philosophical fragments that have directly inspired me; I wanted each selection to "smell of the desert" and to inebriate with its fragrance. Sufi talk or instruction is never linear; Sufi poets and sheikhs will try almost anything to shock their listeners awake, will swerve from the highest philosophy to the fragment of a great ode of Hafiz or Rumi, to a story in yesterday's newspaper, to a joke from Nasrudin. I remember hearing one old Sheikh from the Mevlevi order speak in Paris for two hours and keep everyone preternaturally awake because everything he said was clear, fierce, and vivid—and no one had the slightest idea what he would come up with next. It was like listening to life itself at its most exciting, precarious, and transformatory. I have tried to maintain this electric flow by alternating throughout the anthology poems and fragments of prose, stories with flights of ecstatic philosophy, jokes with diamantine definitions of awareness. I want to invite the reader to stay totally alert and to participate in the making of this anthology by diving deeply into its charged silences and empty spaces filled with the perfume of the desert wind.

There is a structure to *Perfume of the Desert*. It is really a five-part mystical symphony in words that I have designed to take the "listener" from the soul's first awakening to God through all the splendors and rigors of its journey through the Desert of God to the glory and stability of union with the Beloved. Each part has a simple introduction that will initiate the reader into the main themes of what is to follow. In each section the selections are placed in a "musical" order that mirrors what I have come to understand of the journey into love itself. I hope to communicate the authentic rhythm of awakening, with its alternating, mutually illuminating periods of expansion and contraction, passion and discipline, ecstasy and integration.

Whatever path you are on, let these Sufi heart friends and their words and visions take you deeper into your heart, set you afire with holy passion for the Absolute, awaken you to the sacred necessity of suffering, ennoble your acceptance of ordeal, humble your power of adoration. And with their help and the grace of God, may we all come to serve the Real as they do—with the rapture and precision of the One whom Love has killed and remade!

Introduction

BY ERYK HANUT

All books that deal with the desert—whether they are of a spiritual interest or not—begin with the same question: "What is a desert?" None I have ever read succeeds in giving a reply.

I grew up in cities, cold cities, in the North of Europe. But I have also known zones of different sizes that were virgin of all human occupation: kilometers of lavender fields, run wild, at the place where Provence becomes the Alps; the Sierra Madre in Spain; the plains west of Holland, where the blue eggs of gulls rest on the ground; the jagged cliffs of the Northern California coast; the humid jungle of Hana, bristling with pink haliconias, ready to bite; the vast sea of sand dotted with surreally green palm trees and temple ruins that stretches from Madras to the Indian Ocean. I have truly loved each landscape. In different ways, undoubtedly, but with a passion the lost years have no doubt embellished.

No one can be prepared for the desert. Like a serious illness, it attacks you by surprise, rubbling to nothing all your physical and moral resistance. If I attempted a definition of *desert*—idiotic thought—it would consist only of innumerable repetitions of the one word: "Light."

Light — Light — Light. . . .

Even when it becomes pink, at dusk, the desert light is as fierce as ever. It goes on invading you. It kills car motors and burns the skin off faces. Suddenly it goes and, for a few hours, a vast cold takes its place. Perhaps everyone, on leaving the desert, should undergo a ritual of purification. I wrote "purification" but what I really mean is "exorcism," because it is essentially a question of possession. Or of passion, which amounts to the same thing.

In the petrified forest of Arizona, on the cliffs of Zion, or in the Sonoran, squeezed between two small boulders like a lizard, taking photos, I have sometimes secretly thought I would stay there forever, and never leave.

The desert does not seem to sleep. Life doesn't define itself there in the ways it does elsewhere. It is not vegetable or animal or mineral, but a little of all three at once. It is life that needs all faces to survive. A saguaro cactus is not far from being a snake, or a snake from a burning rock. Everything — because it battles against the same ancient enemy — has come to look like everything else.

This immense harshness is a twin of purity. It is today what the planet was when nothing and no one walked on it. It has something about it of Atlantis or Shangri-La. The first Fathers of the Christian Church ran into it to be clothed in its mystery. Corruption doesn't exist there, and what we take for solitude is perhaps another name for innocence.

The Sufis, I am certain, polished their philosophy in the wind of the desert. The plants that grow there are fragrant, for the most part. Pines and aloes survive there. The odor of their leaves, rubbed between two fingers—the perfume of the desert—is concentrated, distilled to a quintessence, sublimed perhaps by the absence of water. This is how Sufis speak, and this is how their voices come across in this book. Concentratedly, without ornament. In a fierce way, too noble for consolation. "It is colorless and one. It is eternal and invisible. The winds of change never break over it."

How could they have developed a less stripped-back, austere, stinging tradition in an environment like this, surrounded as they often were by the Eternal Desert, least flattering of mirrors? "Don't be amazed at those murdered in the dust at the Friend's door. Be amazed at how anyone can survive. . . ."

EPIGRAPHS

Sufism means that God causes you to die to yourself and be united to Him.

—Junayd

Sufism means that you possess nothing and nothing possesses you.

—Summun

The Sufis are people who have preferred God to everything, so that God has preferred them to everything.

—Dhu al-Nun

The Sufi bows down before none but God.

—Traditional

You are a Sufi when your heart is as soft and as warm as wool.

—Traditional

A Sufi is not concerned with patched cloak and prayer carpet. A Sufi is not concerned with the convention and custom of being a Sufi. A Sufi is one who is not.

—Kharaqani

Sufism is a way of life. It is neither a religion nor a philosophy. There are Hindu Sufis, Muslim Sufis, Christian Sufis . . . we do not belong to any country or any denomination but we work always according to the need of the people of the time.

—Bhai Sahib

OPENING PRAYER

GIVE ME LIGHT

O God, give me light in my heart and light in my tongue and light in my hearing and light in my seeing and light in my feeling and light in every part of my body and light before me and light behind me. Give me, I beg you, light on my right hand and light on my left hand and light above me and light beneath me. O Lord, make light grow within me and give me light and illuminate me.

—The Prophet

✦

PART I

*The
Summons*

$\mathcal{T}$HE SUMMONS

The great journey of the soul to Union begins with the soul's awakening in wonder to its divine nature and its response to the summons of love that is always sounding to it from all sides of the cosmos. One of Rumi's greatest odes begins:

Each moment from all sides rushes to us
The summons to Love.
Do you want to come with us?
This is not the time to stay at home
But to go out and give yourself to the garden. . . .

In Surat 7:171 of the Koran, Allah addresses the whole of not-yet-created humanity with the words "Am I not your Lord?" Humanity is said to have responded, "Yes, we witness it." Sufi mystics call this "witnessing" the Pact of Alast. For them it proves the essential divinity and immortality of every soul and that the journey of the soul to Union is also a journey to Origin. Dhu al-Nun, a great early Sufi saint, defined the "perfect person" as "one who is as he was before he was as he was."

There are innumerable ways in which this "summons" can be heard, perhaps as many ways as there are people. Some hear it in dreams or in an outbreak of visions that explode what they understood before about reality; some meet the Beloved first in the agony and revelation of human love; some are unnerved by loss or disease or bankruptcy or betrayal into re-examining everything in the light of Eternity. For some, love summons them in the disguise of a teacher; for others, love calls to them from the heart of Beethoven's *Missa Solemnis*, or from an open rose, or in the leap of a dolphin.

The ways of receiving the summons will differ and so will the responses. Perhaps only a handful will do what the true seeker does when love's call is heard — reorganize his or her whole life to try and absorb more and more of what love is saying. To begin what the Sufis call the first journey — the journey to God — you have to take the summons seriously, recognize its sacred demand on you to transform your life and being, and turn your heart wholly towards the Beloved. No one can begin to do this powerfully without constant, daily practice — of prayer, of meditation and contemplation, of loving service. For only practice can start to wear down the "seventy thousand veils between the self and the Self, between human and divine consciousness."

Those who do allow themselves to dare to turn to love will be infinitely rewarded. They will be rewarded with nothing less than the ultimate truth about human life — that it is divine and surrounded and infused by the Eternal. They will come to know that their true home is not in time, but in Eternity. They will enter in time the supreme mysteries. They will come to know, in the end, that the voice of love that is "rushing from all sides each moment" is the voice of their innermost identity and that they are starting to travel towards themselves. Listen again to Rumi:

Before any garden or grape or wine existed
Our soul was drunk on eternal wine.
In the Baghdad of Eternity, we all proclaimed ecstatically:
"I am the Supreme Reality!"

SOMETHING SANG

The lute began. . .
My heart snapped its chains.
Something sang from the strings —
"Wounded crazy one. . .come!"

—Rumi

COME, COME, WHOEVER YOU ARE

Come, come, whoever you are —
Wanderer, worshiper, lover of leaving —
What does it matter?
Ours is not a caravan of despair.
Come, even if you have broken your vows
A hundred times —
Come, come again, come.

—Rumi

7

EVEN AN ANIMAL IS SHAKEN

One day I was traveling with some devout companions towards the Hejaz in Arabia. There was however a scoffer among us, a man who dismissed all mystical talk as "rubbish." One evening, near Beni Hilal Oasis, a boy started to sing. He sang with such exalted sweetness that the scoffer's camel started to dance and then galloped off into the desert.

I turned to the scoffer and said "Sir, you remain unmoved, yet the boy's singing has shaken even an animal."

—Sadi

HELP ME, LORD

Lashed by desire
I roamed the streets of Good and Evil.
What did I gain? Nothing —
The fire of desire grew only fiercer.
As long as life goes on breathing in me
Help me, Lord —
You alone hear my prayer.

—Sheikh Ansari

WITHOUT YOUR MERCY

From the consequences of what I have done,
From the dangers of the future,
I see no way out.
Lord, I am terrified of the evil in me.
Teach me how to save myself
From the traps of self.
Take me by the hand —
Without Your mercy
I have nothing to turn to.

—Sheikh Ansari

TAKE ME FROM MISERY TO JOY

O Lord! I have squandered my life
Wounded my soul
Done everything in my power
To delight the Evil One.
Whether I go on living,
Or not, does not matter.
Accept my repentance, forgive my sins,
Take me from misery to joy.

—Sheikh Ansari

DO ALL YOU CAN

In the dead of night, a Sufi began to weep.
He said, "This world is like a closed coffin, in which
We are shut and in which, through our ignorance,
We spend our lives in folly and desolation.
When Death comes to open the lid of the coffin,
Each one who has wings will fly off to Eternity,
But those without will remain locked in the coffin.
So, my friends, before the lid of this coffin is taken off,
Do all you can to become a bird of the Way to God;
Do all you can to develop your wings and your feathers."

—Attar

10

To Reach God

The Sufi is the person who intends from the very beginning to reach God, the Creative Truth. Until he has found that Truth, he does not rest or pay attention to anyone.

For your sake, I hurry over land and water.
For your sake, I cross the desert and split the mountain in two,
And turn my face from all things,
Until the time I reach the place
Where I am alone with You.

—Hallaj

Your Ancient Home

You may have lived many years in a city,
But as soon as you fall asleep,
Another city rears in your mind
Full of its own good and evil
And your own city—the one you lived in for years—
Vanishes completely from your memory.
You do not say, "I am a stranger here; this is not my city."
You think you have always lived there.
You think you were born and bred there.

Are you amazed, then, that your soul
Does not remember its ancient home?
How could she remember?
She is wrapped in the sleep of this world
Like a star shrouded by clouds,
And she has tramped through so many cities,
And the dust that darkens her vision
Has not yet been swept away.

—Rumi

DON'T BOAST

Kabir, don't boast about your body,
That skin-sheet stuffed with bones;
Princes who rode regal stallions
Under umbrellas of gold
Now lie folded in earth.

Kabir, don't boast
About your gorgeous palaces;
Today or tomorrow
The ground will be your bed
And grass smother your head.

12

Don't boast about your luck, Kabir,
And despise the desperate:
Your ship's still out at sea —
Who knows its fate?

Kabir, don't boast
Of your beauty and youth:
Today or tomorrow
You'll have to abandon them
Like a serpent its own skin.

—Kabir

REBUKED BY A CAMEL-DRIVER

One night in the desert of Faid, I fell asleep. A camel driver shook me awake and said, "Get up now! The bell is ringing! Do you want to be left behind? I too would like to sleep like you but the desert stretches ahead. How will you reach the end of the journey if you sleep when the drum of departure beats?"

Happy are those who have packed their bags before the beat of the drum! Those asleep by the road do not lift their heads and the caravan passes out of sight.

The one who was awake early traveled furthest; what use is waking up when the caravan has gone?

Now is the time to sow the seeds of the harvest you want to reap. Do not go bankrupt to the Resurrection; sitting in bitter regret is useless. The stock you have already you can increase, but no profit grows on stock you consume yourself.

Strive now, when the water does not reach beyond your waist; do not wait until the flood has raced over your head.

Listen to the advice of the wise today, for tomorrow the Angel of Death will question you sternly. Value your soul as priceless, for a cage without a bird has no value. Do not waste your time in grief and regret; opportunity is precious and time is a sword.

—Sadi

THE PACT OF ALAST

The Pact of Alast (*Alastu bi-Rabbikum?*—"Am I not your Lord?") concerned all beings and was addressed to all, and all recognized the sovereignty of God. However, as only man possessed the faculty of perfect consciousness and because it was to him that the teaching of the names and attributes had been conferred, it was man, then, who was the holder of the true Consciousness.

We were made for Your love, since pre-eternity.

Since then, we have been drunk, in love, aware.
Before the creation of the world and of Adam,
We were Your companions at the Feast of Love.

—Lahiji

BE A PASSERBY

Be in this world as if you are a traveler, a passerby, with your clothes and shoes full of dust. Sometimes you will sit under the shade of a tree, sometimes you will walk in the desert. Be a passerby always, for this world is not your home.

—A Hadith of the Prophet

THE THINGS OF THIS WORLD

Someone once asked the Holy Prophet,
"What do you have to say
About the things of this world?"
The Prophet said, "What can I say about them?
They are won only through bitter labor,

15

Kept only through incessant vigilance,
And abandoned with regret."

—Sheikh Ansari

THE PATH OF TRUTH

A man who wished to be accepted as a disciple said to Dhu al-Nun, "I want to enroll in the Path of Truth beyond anything else in the world."

This is what Dhu al-Nun told him: "You can accompany our caravan only if you first accept two things. One is that you will be compelled to do things that you do not want to do. The other is that you will not be allowed to do things which you want to do. 'Wanting' is what stands between human beings and the Path of Truth."

—Dhu al-Nun

THE OLD HAG

Once Jesus saw the world revealed in the form of a hideous old hag. He asked her how many husbands she had had. "I lost count," she replied. Then he asked her whether they had died or been divorced. She said she had murdered them all.

"What amazes me," he said, "is the number of fools who see what you have done to others and still want you."

—Ghazali

THE OLD WITCH

The world is cunning like an old witch
And her tricks are limitless.
She has trapped us in her nets —
Very few ever escape.
Never rely on your own strength;
You cannot free yourself on your own.
Cry out to God, and cling to Him.

Never boast, "I will fight against the world!
I will never be the victim of her games!
I will live in peace
And never give in to her ruses!"
Even if you resist her for two hundred years,
In the end, believe me,
You will be conquered.

On the Day of Resurrection

Everyone will howl with grief
Because of the witch and her tricks.
The only happy soul is the one
Who detaches itself quickly from her
And never looks at her with longing.
He knows she is a dangerous reptile and flees —

As fast as he can, on the wings of prayer,
And adoration, and fasting — to the world beyond.
No one has ever escaped the Dragon
Except the one who takes refuge in Allah.

—Sultan Valad

LET GO OF THE BRANCH

A man was chased off a cliff by a tiger. He fell, and just managed to hold onto a branch. Six feet above him stood the tiger, snarling. A hundred feet below, a violent sea lashed fierce-looking rocks. To his horror, he noticed that the branch he was clutching was being gnawed at its root by two rats. Seeing he was doomed, he cried out, "O Lord, save me!"

He heard a Voice reply, "Of course, I will save you. But first, let go of the branch!"

—Traditional Sufi story

The Pearl

Shibli sought out Junayd as a teacher and said to him, "Many people have informed me that you are a supreme expert on the pearls of awakening and divine wisdom. Either give me one of these pearls or sell one to me."

Junayd smiled. "If I sell you one, you won't be able to pay the price; if I give you one, coming by it so easily will drive you to undervalue it. Do like me; dive headfirst into the Sea. If you wait patiently, you will obtain your Pearl."

—Junayd

Run toward Him

Pre-eternity came from God, the "Yes" from you.
He drew this "Yes" from you without mouth or lips.

When the order, "All descend!" was given to souls,
At that moment they left to find bodies.

God sent souls from heaven to reveal a secret:
All the cries of "Yes" are not alike.

Some are firm, some weak; some just, some mistaken;
Some are wise and intelligent, others simply conformist.

The "Yes" of the wise is separated from others
By the distance between Afghanistan and Turkey.

The Spirits sent from God entered into subtle bodies,
Laughing, like water pouring into a pitcher.

Then, they left this subtle dwelling
And entered into material bodies.

Why did the unconditioned fall into this condition?
To perfect itself, to obey God's orders in His absence

And to win deeper peace after each act of submission.
Stay humble in this deceiving world, live in the fear of God.

To have faith in absence and to obey God here below
Is more precious than obeying God in His presence.

Does a slave revolt when the King arrives with his army?
No, he shivers with fear, and quickly submits to Him.

How can such a servile act have any merit?
When the King is present, freedom does not exist,

And heartfelt obedience has no value at all.
It is at the time of absence that it is essential,

With all your powers, to practice obedience.
Then is the time religious practices have meaning

Because you live shaken between fear and hope.

Yet, despite all difficulties, you shoulder your duty;

Because of the passionate hope that inspires you,
You abandon what is tangible for what you are waiting for

And with all your strength, trust in a promise.
You bear a thousand sufferings in the hope

You will arrive at Resurrection Day with a pure face.
You live a hard life, so you can enjoy a sweet death.

You leave the dazzle of the world, for love of faith.
Do you know why God values man more than the angels?

Because, despite all terrors, he runs towards Him.

—Sultan Valad

HURRY TO THE SOURCE

Hidden behind the veil of mystery, Beauty is eternally free from the slightest stain of imperfection. From the atoms of the world, He created a multitude of mirrors; into each one of them He cast the image of His Face; to the awakened eye, anything that appears beautiful is only a reflection of that Face.

Now that you have seen the reflection, hurry to its Source; in that primordial Light the reflection vanishes completely. Do not linger far from that primal Source; when the reflection fades, you will be lost in darkness. The reflection is as transient as the smile of a rose; if you want permanence, turn toward the Source; if you want fidelity, look to the Mine of faithfulness. Why tear your soul apart over something here one moment and gone the next?

—Jami

THE TOUCHSTONE

The touchstone of God cannot fail:
The fake never get past it;
Only he will stand the test
Who, alive, knows how to die.

—Kabir

NOW SEE THE SEA

No one who has passed away from the world, Mohammed said,
Feels anguish and regret for having died.

No, he feels pain for having missed a supreme chance
And weeps, "Why did I not make death my goal—
Death that is the treasure-house of all true wonders?
Why did I go on seeing double and fix my gaze
On ghosts that just dissolved when my hour came?"
The grief of the dead is not because of death,
But because they were obsessed by forms that die,
And never saw that all this foam is moved by the Sea.
The Sea has thrown its foam-flakes on the shore—
If you want to see them, go to any cemetery
And say to them, "Where is your frantic swirling now?"
You will, if you listen, hear them answer silently,
"Ask your question of the Sea, and not of us."
How, after all, could foam fly without a wave?
How could dust swirl upwards without the wind?
You have seen the dust, now dare to see the wind;
You have seen the foam, now see the Sea of Creative Energy.

—Rumi

YOU ARE THE VEIL

Know this: you yourself are the veil which hides you from you. Know also that you cannot reach God through yourself; you reach Him through Him. When God graces you the vision of reaching Him, He summons you to seek for Him and you do.

—Junayd

MY SWAN, LET US FLY

My swan, let us fly to that land
Where your Beloved lives forever.

That land has an up-ended well
Whose mouth, narrow as a thread,
The married soul draws water from
Without a rope or pitcher.

My swan, let us fly to that land
Where your Beloved lives forever.

Clouds never cluster there,
Yet it goes on and on raining.
Don't keep squatting outside in the yard—
Come in! Get drenched without a body!

My swan, let us fly to that land
Where your Beloved lives forever.

That land is always soaked in moonlight;

Darkness can never come near it.
It is flooded always with the dazzle
Of not one, but a million suns.

My swan, let us fly to that land
Where your Beloved lives forever.

— Kabir

THE ONES WHO ATTAIN THE ONE

One day, Jesus saw a group of people squatting disconsolately on a wall, by the side of the road. He asked them, "Why do you look so miserable?"

They groaned, "The fear of Hell has made us like this."

Jesus went on his way, and came to another group, who were also sitting dejectedly by the side of the road. He asked them, "Why are you so unhappy?"

They wept, "The longing for Paradise has made us like this."

Jesus went on walking, until He came to a third group. These were people who had evidently suffered a great deal, but their faces were bright with joy.

Jesus asked them, "What has made you so joyful?"

They smiled, "The Spirit of Truth itself. We have seen Reality, and turned away from all lesser goals."

25

Jesus said, "People like these are the ones who attain the One. On the Day of Reckoning, it will be people like these who stand in the Presence of God."

—Ghazali

UNTIL THE RAY OF HIS LOVE FLASHES OUT

No one can find the way to Him by his own strength;
Whoever walks towards Him walks with His foot.
Until the ray of His love flashes out to guide the soul,
It does not set out to see the love of His Face.
My heart is not shaken by the slightest passion for Him
Until a passion flames from Him and works upon my heart.
Since I learnt that the All-Glorious One longs for me,
Longing for Him has not left me for a moment.

—Maghribi

THE MYSTERY OF HIM

What is the most potent in the heart of the mystic while he is at prayer is his awareness of the mystery of Him in whose Presence he is, the power of Him for whom he is looking, and the love of Him who graces him such tender and direct familiarity with Himself. He is conscious of these until he has finished praying and leaves with a face so transfigured that his friends would not recognize him, because of the awe he feels at the majesty of God.

—Muhasibi

PRACTICE THE ONE

A young boy was sent to school. He began his lessons with the other children, and the first lesson the teacher set him was the straight line, the figure "one." But while the others went on progressing, this child continued writing the same figure.

After two or three days the teacher came to him and said, "Have you finished your lesson?"

He said, "No, I'm still writing 'one.'" He went on doing the same thing, and when at the end of the week the teacher asked him again he said, "I have not yet finished it."

The teacher thought he was an idiot and should be sent away, as he could not or did not want to learn. At home the child continued with the same exercise and the parents also became tired and disgusted. He simply said, "I have not yet learned it, I am learning it. When I have finished I shall take the other lessons."

The parents said, "The other children are going on further, your school has abandoned you and you do not show any progress; we are tired of you." And the boy thought sadly that as he had displeased his parents too he had better leave home. So he went into the desert and lived on fruits and nuts.

After a long time he returned to his old school. And when he saw the teacher he said to him, "I think I have learned it. See if I have. Shall I write on this wall?" And when he made his sign the wall split in two.

—Hazrat Inayat Khan

❖

PART II

*The
Inner Secret*

$\mathcal{T}$HE INNER SECRET

As the seeker deepens her experience of the nature of God and of the soul, an astounding secret starts to derange her—she realizes that what she has read in the great mystical books of every tradition is not poetry, or enthusiastic exaggeration, but a literal, and all-shattering truth: that she and the Beloved are not separate but one and that the One she is looking for is also looking for her. This inner secret of identity with the Absolute has many sides to it, and slowly, miraculously, each one of these sides is lit up for the seeker, in the light of the heart, until she realizes, with a certainty beyond "faith" or any possible formulation in words, that the entire creation is one with the Creator, that everything is held together by the force of love, that every atom is drunk on this love, and that the universe that before seemed so orderly is in fact always reeling in drunken, ecstatic dance. She comes to know what Shabistari means when he says, "Under the veil of every atom is hidden / The ravishing face of the Beauty of the Beloved!"

As the implications of this secret start to expand in the seeker's heart and mind—through a constant practice of prayer, meditation, and service and through revelation after revelation—the seeker's own passion for the quest grows more and more ardent.

The more she allows the glory of the secret to awaken and inform her, the more passionate her love for the Beloved grows until it consumes her entire life and burns under every thought and emotion.

Nothing is more important at this stage, so all the greatest Sufi mystics tell us, than to observe as precisely as possible all the rigors of virtue and all our obligations and duties towards others. A very solid cup has to be prepared to hold the increasingly burning wine of gnosis, and this solid cup can only be created in us by a desire to purify ourselves of every habit, disordered appetite, and fantasy that keeps us slaves to ourselves.

Coming to know the "inner secret," then, necessitates a choice to undergo the first great purification on the Path—that of the senses—which clarifies the seeker's being and makes it more and more transparent to love's work. In this purification, the essential labor is one of humility and longing. The Sufi lovers of the Beloved tell us baldly that we must, for our own sakes, always keep on our knees before the majesty of God and always dare to keep up in our hearts a constant stream of longing for the Beloved, however painful that might sometimes be. Without humility, revelation itself can be a source of ignorance because it makes its receiver vain. Longing is both the anguish that burns away the veils of separation between the soul and God and the thread that guides us deeper and deeper within ourselves to where love is waiting, always, to take us further into its mystery.

GOD DEPOSITED WITHIN HUMAN BEINGS

God deposited within human beings knowledge of all things, and then blocked them from perceiving it; this is one of the divine mysteries that reason denies totally and thinks impossible.

The nearness of the mystery to those who do not know it is like God's nearness to His servant, as proclaimed in His words, "We are nearer to Him than you, but you do not see" (Koran 56:83) and His words, "We are nearer to Him than His jugular vein" (Koran 50:16). Despite this nearness, the servant does not perceive or know anything; no one can know what is within himself until it is revealed to him moment by moment.

—Ibn Arabi

THE BIRD ON THIS BODY TREE

There is a bird on this body tree
That dances in the ecstasy of life.
No one knows where it is,
And who could ever know
What its music means?
It nests where branches cast deep shadow;
It comes in the dusk and flies away at dawn
And never says a word of what it intends.

No one can tell me anything
About this bird that sings in my blood.
It isn't colored or colorless;
It doesn't have a form, or outline;
It sits always in the shadow of love.
It lives within the Unreachable, the Boundless, the Eternal
And no one can tell when it comes or when it goes.

Kabir says, "Fellow seeker,
The mystery of this bird
Is marvelous and profound.
Be wise; struggle to know
Where this bird comes to rest."

—Kabir

THE SECOND BIRTH

You are a mine whose soil is mixed with silver.
The silver is hidden in the mine;
The soil is visible, like the body
And the silver, like the soul, is hidden.
Extract the silver from the soil;
The soil is worthless and thrown aside.
The value of the soil comes from the silver.

Without it, it is only dirt.
And although this dirt comes out of the mine
At the same time as the silver,
It doesn't acquire the same value.
If it doesn't escape from itself,
It will remain useless and sterile.
It will be good for nothing
And never be forged into a precious cup.

Think of an oyster you fish out of the sea
That hasn't given birth to a pearl —
What use is it? Who wants to buy it?
Its value will not appear to any eyes,
However experienced they may be.
You must, then, give birth to yourself a second time
Like silver and gold that are born from earth
And free yourself from all danger
And live in peace under God's protection. . . .
When the soil of the mine is thrown in the furnace
It melts and transmutes and becomes precious.
You, too, if you are a real seeker, must melt away

Through the passion of the fire of love
In the furnace of absolute sincerity.
How else can you free yourself from the veils
Of your existence and become drunk on God?
Yes, you must be born twice, once from your mother,

And the second time, from yourself.
You have passed already through the first birth,
Now strive to attain the second
So you can know the secret of Union.
Dedicate your soul to the path of Reality
So you can receive the help and teaching of God.

—Sultan Valad

WHETHER YOUR DESTINY IS GLORY OR DISGRACE

Whether your destiny is glory or disgrace,
Purify yourself of hatred and love of self.
Polish your mirror, and that sublime Beauty
From the regions of mystery
Will flame out in your heart
As it did for the saints and prophets.
Then, with your heart on fire with that Splendor,
The secret of the Beloved will no longer be hidden.

—Jami

THE WORLD IS NEVER FAR FROM HIM

He who is perfect in the Path of Faith
Will never be deceived by Adam's clay:
He will always see the Light in Adam —
Its brilliance will not remain a secret.

In stone, wood, straw, or mountain
He will at all times see nothing but God.
Didn't Bayazid himself see God in all things?
He saw the Face of God in the tiniest leaf.

The world is never far from Him:
Could its perfume stray far from the rosegarden?
He who is deprived of the sense of smell
Cannot distinguish fragrances
Just as the stream-bed isn't conscious
Of the water always flowing through it.

If I revealed any more about these things
The two worlds would disappear
And I would become His enemy
And he would light a fire in my soul and body.

—Sultan Valad

THE TRUE NAMES

Those who know say that the person who wants to know the Divine Essence through names, attributes, and acts is like the dreamer who, in sleep, sees images that are not real. Those who know the true names, attributes, and actions of God are those who have reached through the way of mystic vision an understanding of the Essence and who then descend to the level of the names and attributes. They have understood that it is the Absolute Essence of God that is manifesting itself, every moment, under the appearance of a name and attribute. They are wide awake and see the reality of things.

—Lahiji

MY TRUE SERVANT

Man is my secret and I am his. The inner knowledge of the spiritual essence is a secret of my secrets. Only I placed this in the heart of my true servant, and no one can know his state but I.

—A Hadith of the Prophet

THIS IS YOUR HEART

I saw God on the streets of the hidden with something in His hand. I said, "My Lord, what is it that you are holding?"

He said, "Your heart."

I said, "Does my heart have such a station that it lies in Your hand?"

He gazed at my heart, and it looked like something that was folded up. He smoothed and spread it out, and my heart covered the space from the Throne to the earth. He said, "This is your heart, and it is the most vast thing in existence." Then He took my heart to the angelic regions and I went with Him, until I reached the treasures of the hidden in the hidden.

—Ruzbihan Baqli

THE SECRET

How could I ever express the Secret?
If I say He is within me
The entire universe hangs its head in shame
Yet if I say He is outside me
I know I'm a liar.
He makes the inner world and the outer One:
Conscious, Unconscious —both are His footstools.

He is neither manifest nor hidden;
He is neither revealed, nor unrevealed.
There are no words to describe what He is.

—Kabir

ONE LIGHT

What are "I" and "You"?
Just lattices
In the niches of a lamp
Through which the One Light radiates.

"I" and "You" are the veil
Between heaven and earth;
Lift this veil and you will see
How all sects and religions are one.

Lift this veil and you will ask —
When "I" and "You" do not exist
What is mosque?
What is synagogue?
What is fire temple?

—Shabistari

THOSE WHO KNOW

Those who know
The million million colors and forms
Spring from one color, one form,
Pay no attention whatsoever
To castes or divisions.

Those who do not recognize God
Die;
Those who give their hearts
To anything but God
Die;
Those who enthuse about the Scriptures
They die too —
They adore the words
But never realize
The Spirit behind them.

All they go about doing, in fact,
Is applying makeup
To eyes already blind with prejudice —
O Sheikh Tazi, realize
Once and for all
The Lord of Eternity lives
In every pot.

— Kabir

IN MY KNOWING HIM, I CREATE HIM

He praises me, and I praise Him.
He worships me, and I worship Him.
How can He be independent
When I help and assist Him?
In my knowing Him, I create Him.

—Ibn Arabi

THE SOUL THAT DOES NOT LIVE IN GOD
IS NOT ALIVE

Spring makes red and white flowers appear on the trees,
But the spring that is the origin of colors is colorless.

Understand what I have said, and give up all talk;
Run to the Origin without color and unite yourself to it.

Annihilate yourself before the One Existence
So that thousands of worlds leap out of you

And your pure existence flames out of itself
And goes on and on birthing different forms.

Of course, none of these forms will last.

44

Happy is the one who knows this mystery!

Happy is he who gives his life to know this!
He leaves this house for another, far more radiant.

You cannot understand this mystery through reason;
The Way to Knowledge winds through suffering and torment.

If you do not feel pain, you do not look for healing.
The soul that does not live in God is not alive.

She seems like a soul, but does not deserve the name:
She has not been made alive by the Beloved.

The soul is given life by the four elements
Like a lamp that burns through the night:

This light is from oil and wick, it is not eternal.
While the oil exists, the lamp burns, but then goes out.

The one made alive by God will never die.
He lives through God and not through gold or bread.

God is the Light, the Eternal Source of Lights.
This Light is causeless, as is His fiery radiance.

Like gold, God's value comes from His pure, perfect essence.

—Sultan Valad

WITHIN THIS BODY

Within this body
Are enchanted fields and woods,
The seven seas and the innumerable stars.

Within this body
Are the touchstone and the jeweler.

Within this body
The Eternal keeps singing
And Its spring goes on and on flowing.

Kabir says, "Listen, my friend, listen —
My beloved Lord is within."

—Kabir

THE PEOPLE OF THE HIDDEN LETTER

He said to me, Who are the people of the fire?
I said, The people of the exterior letter.

He said, Who are the people of the garden?
I said, The people of the hidden letter.

He said to me, What is the exterior letter?

46

I said, Knowledge that does not lead to action.

He said, What is the hidden letter?
I said, Knowledge that leads to reality.

He said, What is the action?
I said, Sincerity.

He said, What is reality?
I said, That through which you reveal yourself.

He said to me, What is sincerity?
I said, Turning towards your face.

He said, What is self-revelation?
I said, What you meet in the heart of your lovers.

—Niffari

GIVE UP YOUR PLACE

At the beginning of my mystical search, I knew nothing and so attached myself to the Imam Sayyed Mohammed Nurbaksh. During my second retreat of forty days I saw the Imam in a dream and he asked me, "Can you get up and give your place to someone else?" When I woke up, I thought that since I had made hardly any progress, this dream meant that I should give my place to someone else who could benefit more from the Sheikh's presence.

That evening, I told my dream to the Sheikh and what I had deduced from it. He said to me, "The real interpretation of your dream is this: you must forget yourself and 'give up your place' to the Supreme Reality." These words, which provoked a pain in my heart, marked the beginning of my spiritual evolution.

—Lahiji

SPIRITUAL HUNGER

Spiritual hunger is a living, radiant fire put by God into the hearts of His servants so that their ego can be burned; when it has been burned, this fire then becomes the fire of longing, which never dies, either in this world or the next.

There is no quicker way to God than spiritual hunger; if it travels through solid rock, water gushes forth. Spiritual hunger is essential for the Sufis; it is the showering of God's mercy on them.

—Abu Said Ibn Abi Khayr

THAT SINGLE SIGH

If the eight paradises were revealed in my hut, and if the rulership of the entire world were placed in my hands, I would not give for them that single sigh that arises at dawn from the depths of my soul when I remember my longing for Him.

—Bayazid Bistami

CONCERNING BENEVOLENCE

If you are wise, hunger for the essential truth, for that remains, while all external things pass away. If you have neither knowledge, generosity, or devotion, you are a human being in form alone. If you want to sleep at peace beneath the ground, make tranquil the hearts of beings above it.

Give now of your gold and wealth, for soon it will pass from your grasp. Open the door of your treasure today, for tomorrow the key will not be in your hands.

If you do not want to be in misery on the Day of Judgment, do not forget those who are in misery now. Do not drive the beggar from your door, or you will one day wander desperate before the door of strangers. God protects the one who fears that one day he too might need the help of others. Are you not also a suppliant? Be grateful, and never turn away those that turn in tears to you.

—Sadi

FOUR THINGS TO KNOW

Hatim al-Asamm said, "I have chosen four things to know and discarded all other kinds of knowledge.

"The first is this: I know that my daily bread is apportioned to me and will neither be increased or decreased, so I have stopped trying to add to it.

"Secondly, I know I owe to God a debt which no one else can pay for me, so I am busy about paying it.

"Thirdly, I know that there is someone pursuing me—Death—whom I cannot escape from, so I have prepared myself to meet him.

"Fourth, I know that God is observing me, so I am ashamed to do what I should not."

—Attar

ON GRATITUDE

How could I ever thank my Friend?
No thanks could ever begin to be worthy.
Every hair of my body is a gift from Him;
How could I thank Him for each hair?
Praise that lavish Lord forever
Who from nothing conjures all living beings!
Who could ever describe His goodness?
His infinite glory lays all praise waste.
Look, He has graced you a robe of splendor
From childhood's first cries to old age!
He made you pure in His own image; stay pure.
It is horrible to die blackened by sin.
Never let dust settle on your mirror's shining;
Let it once grow dull and it will never polish.
When you work in the world to earn your living
Do not, for one moment, rely on your own strength.
Self-worshiper, don't you understand anything yet?
It is God alone that gives your arms their power.
If, by your striving, you achieve something good,
Don't claim the credit all for yourself;
It is fate that decides who wins and who loses
And all success streams only from the grace of God.
In this world you never stand by your own strength;
It is the Invisible that sustains you every moment.

—Sadi

51

GUSTS OF FAVOR

I was cured of my disease of skepticism not by systematic demonstration or beautifully crafted argument, but by a light which God threw into my breast. That light is the key to the greater part of knowledge. Whoever imagines that the understanding of divine things rests upon strict and exact proofs has narrowed the wideness of God's mercy.

When the Messenger of God (Peace be upon Him!) was asked about "enlarging" and its meaning in the verse, "Whenever God wills to guide a man, he enlarges his breast for surrender to God," the Prophet said, "It is a light which God throws into the heart." When asked, "What is its sign?" he said, "Withdrawal from the house of deception and return to the house of Eternity."

It was about this light that Muhammed (Peace be upon Him!) said, "God created the creatures in darkness, and then sprinkled upon them some of His light." It is from that light that you must look for intuitive knowledge of divine things. From time to time, that light gushes from the spring of Divine Generosity; you have to watch and wait for it, as the Prophet (Peace be upon Him!) said, "The Lord has gusts of favor; place yourselves in their way."

—Ghazali

The Lights

There are lights which ascend and lights which descend. The ascending lights are the lights of the heart; the descending lights are those of the Throne. The false self is the veil between the Throne and the heart. When this veil is torn and a door opens in the heart, like springs towards like. Light ascends toward light and light descends upon light, and "it is light upon light" (Koran 24:35).

—Najm al-Din Kubra

The Secret of the Journey

Each time the heart sighs for the Throne, the Throne sighs for the heart, so they come to meet. Each time a light ascends from you, a light descends towards you; each time a flame ascends from you an answering flame descends towards you. If their energies are equal, then they meet halfway. But when the substance of light has grown in you, then this makes up a whole in relation to what is of the same nature in Heaven. Then, it is the substance of light in Heaven that longs for you, and is drawn to your light, and it descends towards you. This is the secret of the mystical journey.

—Najm-al-Din Kubra

THE KINGDOM OF DIVINE GLORY

By means of the Divine Lights the heart comes to be so polished that it shines like a polished mirror. When it becomes a mirror like this, you can see in it the reflection of all existing things and the reflection of the Kingdom of God as they really are.

When you see the glory and majesty of God in His Kingdom, then all the lights become one light and your chest brims over with this radiant light. You are now like a person who observes her reflection in a mirror; as you look at yourself, you also see the reflection of everything that is in front of you and behind you.

Now, if a ray of sun strikes the mirror, the entire house will become flooded with light from the meeting of these two lights — the light of the ray of sun and the light of the mirror. The same is true of the heart: when it is polished and luminous, it sees the Kingdom of Divine Glory and the Divine Glory becomes naked to it.

— Hakim al-Tirmidhi

THE CHILD OF THE HEART

The Sufis describe a spiritual state as a "baby" because that "baby" is born in the core of the heart and is nursed and fed and grows there. The heart, like a mother, births, gives suck to, and brings up the child of the heart. Children are taught the various worldly forms of knowledge; the child of the heart is taught inner wisdom. As even an ordinary child is not yet polluted with the sins of the world, so the child of the heart is pure, free from carelessness, selfishness, and doubt. A child's purity appears often in physical beauty; the purity of the heart's child appears in dreams and in the shape of angels. Don't just hope to enter Paradise on the strength of actions; let the gift of Paradise come to you, now and here, through the hands of the child of the heart.

—Jilani

The Secret of the Universe

Non-being is the mirror of Absolute Being.
There, the radiance of Reality is reflected
And grasps its reflection in a second.
Unity is manifest in plurality
Just as, when you count one, it becomes many.
All numbers begin by one,
Yet you can never find their end.
Since Non-being is pure in itself
It is in it that the "hidden treasure" is reflected.
Read the Hadith "I was a hidden treasure"

So you can enter this boundless mystery.
Non-being is the mirror, the world is the reflection,
Man the reflected eye of the Invisible Person.
You are this reflected eye; He is the light of the eye.
And in this eye, His eye sees His own eye.
The world is a man and a man is a world.
When you dive into the abyss of this mystery
You are at once the seer, the eye that sees, and what is seen.
The sacred tradition has affirmed it
And demonstrated it "without eyes or ears" —
Know, then, the entire universe is a mirror.
In each atom nest a hundred flaming suns:
Cleave the heart of single drop of water —
A hundred pure oceans will gush out.
Examine a single grain of dust —
A thousand Adams will arise.
In its limbs, a fly is like an elephant;
In its qualities, a drop of rain is like the Nile.
The entire universe is hidden
In the heart of a millet grain;
The heart of a barleycorn
Is richer than a hundred harvests.
In the wing of a fly
Streams the ocean of Life;
In the pupil of the eye
An endless heaven opens.

However tiny the grain of the heart may be,
The Lord of all the world has made his dwelling there.
There the two worlds have been made one:
The Tempter manifests God's terrible majesty,
And Adam His divine beauty.
Contemplate the world as it is,
Angels interweave with devils, Satan with Gabriel.
Everything is assembled like a seed and its fruit —
The unbeliever with the believer, the loyal with the disloyal.
Everything is united on the diamond-point of the present —
The cycles and seasons, the day, the month, the year,
The world without beginning and the world without end.
The mission of Jesus coincides with the creation of Adam:
From each point of this always-revolving circle
Thousands of forms are born.
In its turning, every point is
Sometimes a center, sometimes a circumference.
If you were to remove one atom from its place,
The entire universe would crumble in ruin.
The All is a vertiginous whirlwind, yet no part of it
Finds itself beyond the limits of contingency,
For Emanation keeps everything in dependence.
Everything is desperate
From being separated from the All;
Everything travels ceaselessly and yet stays in its place;
Everything is always in movement and yet always at peace —

Never beginning, and never ending.
Everything knows its essence and this is why
Everything is always racing toward the Throne.
Under the veil of every atom is hidden
The ravishing beauty of the face of the Beloved!

—Shabistari

O KING, WHO BURNS AWAY THE UNIVERSE

Shabistari tells us that the light of the Essence is not contained in the places of manifestation. How then, he asks, can human reason attain the authentic knowledge of God, since it is compelled to judge things through phenomena? I want to tell you here what happened to me when I was in retreat.

While I was asleep, I saw myself flying in the air and wheeling around a large city, entirely filled with candles and lamps, so luminous that no words can describe it. Suddenly, I started to rise towards the sky and came to the first heaven. I saw that I had become this heaven and experienced extremely strange things. Then I ascended to the second heaven and also became it. There too, I experienced amazing and inexplicable things. I continued like this until I arrived at the seventh heaven. I felt that I was flying in a subtle world and saw the Supreme Reality manifest

58

itself like Absolute Light. Through Its splendor, the wonder It inspired, and Its flashing-out, the entire universe caught fire and everything was burnt away. I also felt this fire and was annihilated. Then, I saw that I had returned to myself and in my ecstasy I recited:

> *O my King, who burns away the universe and gives to each thing a soul,*
> *O You, my burning and my patience, when will I see You one more time?*

—Lahiji

BOTH VEILS MUST GO

One day Rabia was seen running, with fire in one hand and water in the other. They asked her why she was doing this and where she was going. She replied "I am running to light a fire in Heaven and to pour water on the flames of Hell, so that both veils to the Face disappear forever."

—Rabia

I Take Refuge in You

Rabia was once asked, "How did you attain that which you have attained?"

"By often praying, 'I take refuge in You, O God, from everything that distracts me from You, and from every obstacle that prevents me from reaching You.'"

—Rabia

All Things Are Obedient

Omm Ahmad was a holy woman from Egypt who was also a midwife. She never charged for her services but did her work only to please God.

"One winter night," her son tells us, "She ordered me to light the lantern. I told her that we were out of oil. She then ordered me to pour water into the lantern and to remember God. As I did so, the wick caught fire of itself. I was astonished and asked her, 'Mother, is the water really burning?' 'No' she replied, 'but to the one who obeys God, all things are obedient.'"

—Attar

THE WAY OF THE WORLD

"Every single day," Nasrudin proclaimed to his wife, "I am more and more amazed at the marvelously efficient way this world is organized, and for the best for humankind."

"Give me an example," said his wife.

"Take camels. Why do you imagine they have no wings?"

"I have no idea."

"It's easy—if camels had wings they could squat on housetops and destroy our peace by stamping about up there and spitting their cud down at us!"

—Nasrudin

FEAR IS ALL YOU NEED

One day, a cruel and vicious king said to Nasrudin, "I am going to have you hanged, drawn, and quartered if you do not prove that you have insights as deep as those attributed to you."

At once, Nasrudin said, "I can see a vast golden bird in the sky when I look up, and demons howling and dancing in the earth when I look down."

"How can you do this?"

"Fear," said Nasrudin, "is all you need."

—Nasrudin

DONKEYS

Nasrudin used to take his donkey across a frontier every day, loaded with baskets full of straw. Because he freely confessed to being a smuggler when he came home every night, the frontier guards would search him again and again. They used to strip him, sift the straw, steep it in water, sometimes even burn it. Meanwhile, Nasrudin was becoming more and more wealthy.

Then he retired and went to live in another country. Here one of the frontier guards happened to meet him, years later.

"You can tell me now, Nasrudin," he said. "What on earth were you smuggling all that time when we could never catch you out?"

"Donkeys," said Nasrudin.

—Nasrudin

THE DISCOVERY

I've found something so rare,
So miraculous,
No one can assess
How much it is worth.

It is colorless and One;
It is eternal and indivisible;
The waves of Change never break over it;
It fills every vessel.

It has no weight; it has no price;
No one can ever measure it;
No one can count it;
It cannot be known
Through talk or erudition.
It isn't heavy and it isn't light.
There isn't a touchstone in any world
That can reveal its worth.

I live in it; it lives in me
And we are one, like water
Mingled with water.
The one who knows it
Can never die —
The one who doesn't know it
Dies again and again.

—Kabir

THE SWING

Between the posts of "conscious" and "unconscious"
The mind has strung a swing:
On it hang all beings, all worlds
And it never stops swaying.

Millions of beings sit on it
And the sun and moon also.
Millions of eras come and go
But the swing remains.

Everything swings!
Sky and earth, air and water
And the Beloved Himself
As He comes into form —

Seeing this
Has made Kabir a servant.

—Kabir

❖

PART III

O God,
Grace Me Love of You!

O God, Grace Me Love of You!

The "summons" of the Beloved has been heard and the "inner secret" has started to radiate its fire of knowledge into all aspects of the seeker's mind and heart and life. At this third stage of the quest, the seeker becomes like a dry log immersed in fire; he learns to burn and to want to burn ever more passionately with the ardor of pure love for God.

What has become completely clear to the seeker by now is that the only thing that veils God from him is himself, and that the fastest, most powerful, and most beautiful way of wearing down this false self with all its disastrous vanities and distractions is to fall ever more completely in love with Love. In the fire of Love, all imperfections in the self are slowly burned away and everything cold—or even frozen—and vicious in the self is slowly healed.

Everything must be given to the pursuit of so demanding and overwhelming a love of Love. Every desire, appetite, passion, thought, emotion has to be fed to this Love, compelled to become one with it. This takes enormously steady inner work—constant heart work—and the greatest help to the seeker at this stage is to keep up a continual river of prayer in the heart, a constant stream of remembrance through saying the Divine Name in every situation and circumstance. Continual remembrance of the Beloved is the key to remaining always in the Presence; constantly invoking the Beloved's help and grace is the key to staying always open to them; constantly pouring out one's heart in praise and gratitude is the key to experiencing the love that is always streaming towards you from the Beloved and is also your own inmost nature.

"Wherever you may be," Rumi tells us in his *Discourses*, "in whatever situation or circumstances, strive to be a lover, and a passionate lover. Once you possess your heart in love, you will always be a lover in the tomb, at the Resurrection, and in Paradise forever and ever."

In this third stage of the journey, the seeker learns how, as in Rumi's beautiful phrase, "to possess the heart in love." Such self-possession initiates the seeker progressively into the glory—what the Sufis call the *kibriya*—of the Beloved. As Rumi tells us, "Adore and love Him with your whole being, and He will reveal to you that each thing in the universe is a vessel full to the brim with wisdom and beauty. Each thing he will show you is one drop from the boundless river of His Infinite Beauty."

Such a vision, the mystics know, drives the heart mad with wonder. As the dazzling gifts of this divine madness become ever clearer to the seeker, he strives with all his being to die more and more completely into the Love that he now knows is the one true

Life and the source of immortal being. Everything in him starts
to cry out with Rumi's great cry:

Give me ecstasy, give me naked wonder, O my Creator!
Give birth to the Beloved in me, and let this lover die.
Let a thousand wrangling desires become one Love.

O GOD, GRACE ME LOVE OF YOU!

The Prophet taught the following prayer to his companions:

"O God, grace me love of You, and to love those who love You, and to love whatever brings me nearer to You.

O God, make your love more precious to me than cool water to the thirsty."

—Ghazali

THE ONLY CURE

The source of my suffering and loneliness is deep in my heart.
This is a disease no doctor can cure.
Only Union with the Friend can cure it.

—Rabia

EMPTY ME OF EVERYTHING BUT YOUR LOVE

Lord, send me staggering with the wine
Of Your love!
Ring my feet
With the chains of Your slavery!
Empty me of everything but Your love
And in it destroy and resurrect me!
Any hunger You awaken
Can only end in Feast!

—Sheikh Ansari

DRAW IT NOW FROM ETERNITY'S JAR

Come, come, awaken all true drunkards!
Pour the wine that is Life itself!
O cupbearer of the Eternal Wine,
Draw it now from Eternity's Jar!
This wine doesn't run down the throat
But it looses torrents of words!
Cupbearer, make my soul fragrant as musk,
This noble soul of mine that knows the Invisible!
Pour out the wine for the morning drinkers!
Pour them this subtle and priceless musk!

Pass it around to everyone in the assembly
In the cups of your blazing drunken eyes!
Pass a philter from your eyes to everyone else's
In a way the mouth knows nothing of,
For this is the way cupbearers always offer
The holy and mysterious wine to lovers.
Hurry, the eyes of every atom in Creation
Are famished for this flaming-out of splendor!
Procure for yourself this fragrance of musk
And with it split open the breast of heaven!
The waves of the fragrance of this musk
Drive all Josephs out of their minds forever!

—Rumi

O Love

O Love, O pure deep Love, be here, be now,
Be all—worlds dissolve into your
stainless endless radiance,
Frail living leaves burn with you brighter
than cold stars—
Make me your servant, your breath, your core.

—Rumi

WHEN THE REAL GIVES YOU A HEART

Rabia said, "The mystic is one who asks the Real for a heart. When the Real gives him a heart, immediately he returns it to the Omnipotent and Glorious One. Why? So it can be protected in His hand and hidden from all creatures in His veil."

—Rabia

CERTAIN PROOF

Brothers, my peace is in my aloneness.
My Beloved is alone with me there, always.
I have found nothing in all the worlds
That could match His love,
This love that harrows the sands of my desert.
If I come to die of desire
And my Beloved is still not satisfied,
I would live in eternal despair.

To abandon all that He has fashioned
And hold in the palm of my hand
Certain proof that He loves me —
That is the name and the goal of my search.

—Rabia

THE LORD'S TRUE WORSHIPER

Beloved Lord,
Either I am crazy
Or this world of Yours is.

The very worship You don't care about
Is the one everyone's trapped in —
About the worship You love,
Hardly anyone knows anything.

To love You, love You, and no one else,
That's the worship that delights You.
That is why the soul was parted from You —
To return to You through adoration.

Why get caught in empty formalities?
I sing the glory of my love.
I sing of what I have seen myself.
The one who reaches the rank of Lover
Is the Lord's true worshiper.

—Kabir

TRUE GENEROSITY

Rabia once asked Sofyan Thawri, "What is your definition of generosity?"

He replied, "For the inhabitants of this world, generosity consists in giving away what one has; for those of the world beyond, generosity is to sacrifice one's own soul."

Rabia objected and said that he was wrong. Sofyan then asked her what her definition of generosity was.

"Generosity," she said, "is to worship Him for love of Himself alone, and not for any benefit or reward."

—Rabia

LOVE'S FAMILIAR

What does it mean to be Love's familiar?
To become blood, to swallow your own blood,
To wait at fidelity's door with the dogs. . . .
In weeping, the lover is like the clouds;
In perseverance, like the mountains;
In prostration, like water;
In humility, like dirt in the road.

—Rumi

O LORD

O Lord,
If tomorrow on Judgment Day
You send me to Hell,
I will tell such a secret
That Hell will race from me
Until it is a thousand years away.

O Lord,
Whatever share of this world
You could give to me,
Give it to Your enemies;
Whatever share of the next world
You want to give to me,
Give it to Your friends.
You are enough for me.

O Lord,
If I worship You
From fear of Hell, burn me in Hell.

If I worship You
From hope of Paradise, bar me from its gates.

But if I worship You for Yourself alone
Then grace me forever the splendor of Your Face.

—Rabia

A STORY
ILLUSTRATING THE REALITY
OF LOVE

A young man who loved God turned his face towards the desert. His father, grieved at his absence, could not eat or sleep. A friend of the family railed at the son for his behavior. He could only reply, "My Friend has claimed me as His own; now I can own no other friendship but His. When He unveiled His beauty to me, everything else I saw seemed unreal." Those who love Him cannot care for anyone else; their senses are shut away and bewildered in adoration, their ears are deaf to any reproach.

Without a caravan, they wander through the desert of divine knowledge.

They have no hope of understanding or approval from their fellows for they are the chosen of the elect of God.

—Sadi

What Remains but Drowning?

Love does not live in science and learning
Or in any careful order of pages and letters.
Whatever people chatter about
Is not the Way of Lovers.
The branches of Love are in pre-eternity
Its roots in the post-eternal.
This is a Tree that does not exist
On any supports of heaven or earth.
We have dethroned reason and imprisoned desire,
For the majesty of Divine Love
Cannot live with such fools and their habits.
So long as you hunger after anything,
What you long for will be an idol.
When Love decides to love you back
You will no longer exist.
All sailors totter on planks of fear and hope —
But when "planks" and "sailor" have vanished,
What remains but drowning?
Shams of Tabriz, you are sea and pearl;
The mystery of your being
Is the secret of the Creator.
My Soul, the first time I saw you
My soul heard wonders from your soul.
And when my heart drank water from your fountain
It drowned in you, and the river swept me away.

—Rumi

81

THE WOMAN IN THE DESERT

Once, I met a woman in the desert.

"Where are you from?" I asked her.

"From my homeland."

"Where are you going?"

"To my home."

"Where are your supplies?" I inquired.

"The One who called me graces me what I need because I trust in Him."

"Don't you have any water?"

"Only those who are afraid take water with them."

"Don't you have a donkey or camel? The journey is long."

"I have four different mounts. My first is Resignation and I sit on it whenever God's Providence oppresses me. Then, when harsh times come, I ride upon Patience and exercise forbearance. Then, when I am blessed by Divine Grace, I sit upon the mount of Gratitude and praise God. Whenever I am blessed by God's love, I sit on the stallion of Yearning."

She turned her gaze towards heaven and said, "O Lord, Your love has consumed my soul, driven me out of my home, and made me an aimless wanderer."

The woman started to weep and I asked her why.

"Yearning drags me everywhere and yet my Friend is absent. My heart is driven mad by love and totally indifferent to itself. How can there be any peace anywhere for me?"

I saw from her passion that she was sincere.

"What is the true path to the Transcendent?" I asked her.

"To seek for the Beloved through the heart upon the scales of the Invisible World."

—Abu Muhammed Morta'ash

If You Do Not Burn with Longing

Night and day I played my life away
With those I believed my friends
And now I am terrified.

The palace of my Lord is set so high
My heart trembles at climbing its stairs,
But I cannot be timid now
If I ever hope to win His love.

My heart must cling to Him.
I must throw off all my veils
And meet Him with my whole body.
My eyes must now perform
The ceremony of the lamps of love.

Kabir says, "Listen, my friend—
He who loves, knows.
If you do not burn with longing

For the Beloved,
Don't bother wrapping your body in rich silk;
Don't bother ringing your eyes with kohl."

—Kabir

STORY OF A MOTH AND A CANDLE

Someone said to a moth, "Go, you ridiculous little creature, and make friends with someone of your own kind. How different your love is from the candle's! You are not a salamander—don't hover around the fire. You have to be brave before you can fight. It is absurd to try and embrace as a friend someone you know is your enemy."

"What does it matter if I burn?" the moth replied. "I have love in my heart and the candle's flame is a flower to me. I do not throw myself into the fire of my own will; the chain of His love is around my neck. You can deride my love for my Friend as much as you like; I am happy to be killed at His feet. I burn because He is precious to me and because my destruction may move Him. Do not say to a helpless man from whom the reins have fallen, 'Drive slowly.'"

—Sadi

KILL ME, MY FAITHFUL FRIENDS

Kill me, my faithful friends,
For in my being killed is my life.

Love is that you remain standing
In front of your Beloved
When you are stripped of all your attributes;
Then His attributes become your qualities.

Between me and You, there is only me.
Take away the me, so only You remain.

—Hallaj

ONLY BE SATISFIED WITH ME

My Joy —
My Longing —
My Sanctuary —
My Friend —
My Food for the Journey —
My final End —
You are my spirit, and my hope.
You are my yearning.
You are all my Good.

Without You — O my life, my love —
I would never have wandered
Across these endless countries.
How many gifts and graces You have given me!
How many favors You have fed me from Your hand!
I look for your love in all directions
Then, suddenly, its blessing burns in me.
O Captain of my heart —
Radiant Eye of longing in my breast —
I will never be free of You
As long as I live.
Only be satisfied with me,
Life of my heart,
And I am satisfied.

— Rabia

GOD LOOKS AT HIMSELF THROUGH MAN

Shabistari in his "Rosegarden of Mystery" writes:

By love has appeared everything that exists
And by love that which does not exist appears as existing.

Shabistari means here that man is the eye of the world, and

86

that the world is the reflection of God, and that God Himself is the light of this eye. Man is the eye that looks in the mirror, and just as the mirror reflects the face of the person who is looking into it, the reflection itself possesses an eye; in the same time that the eye looks in the mirror, the reflection of this eye looks back at it. God, who is the eye of man, looks at Himself through man.

This point is extremely subtle: from one perspective, God is the eye of man; from another, man is the eye of the world, because the world and man are one. This man—who is the eye of the world—is called the Perfect Man. Since man is a résumé of everything that exists, he is a world in himself, and the relationship that exists between God and man exists between man and the world.

—Lahiji

Only for You

Life in my body pulses only for You.
My heart beats in resignation to Your will.
If on my grave a clump of grass
Were to grow,
Every blade of it would tremble
With my passion for You.

—Sheikh Ansari

DO NOT BLAME ME

Do not blame me if I gamble
My whole life on your path;
What can I do?
It is all I have.
I would set fire to
The tree of life
If I could snatch one blazing branch
From the flames of your love. . . .

— Khusrawi

AS LONG AS I LIVE

As long as I live I will eat and drink
The grief of loving You.
    I will never give it up to anyone
    Even when I am dead.

Tomorrow
At the Resurrection
    I will walk forward with this violent thirst
    Still storming my head.

— Hamadani

A STORY OF SULTAN MAHMUD
AND HIS LOVE FOR AYAZ

One of his subjects mocked the King of Ghazni behind his back and sneered, "Why is the Sultan so enamored of Ayaz? He isn't even beautiful. How strange that a nightingale should love a rose that isn't either colorful or fragrant?"

This was relayed to Mahmud who said, "My love for Ayaz is for his goodness, not his beauty."

A while later, the King and his court were out riding. In a narrow defile in the desert, one of the camels fell and a chest full of pearls broke open. The King gave a signal that plunder could begin, spurring on his horse. The other horsemen also spurred on their horses and, sweeping past the King, grabbed all the pearls for themselves. The only one who stayed near Mahmud was Ayaz.

"Well, how many pearls did you get?" Mahmud asked him.

"None," Ayaz replied. "I went on walking intently behind you; serving you is all the wealth I could ever want."

—Sadi

ONLY THE LOVERS WILL NOT BE DESTROYED

On the Day of Judgment, the Lord of Wisdom shall demand of the learned, "What did you do with the knowledge and learning I gave you?"

They will reply, "We spent it on your Way."

Then the Lord of Wisdom will say, "You are liars."

The angels also will say, "You are liars."

The Lord of Wisdom will continue, "You say you spent your knowledge and learning 'in my Way.' Nonsense! You spent it in scavenging for applause, trying to pass yourselves off as savants, and wheedling worship from the masses."

The Lord of Magnificence will ask the rich, "What did you do with the wealth I gave you?"

They will say, "We gave it away in your Way."

Then the Lord of Magnificence and his angels will say, "You are lying, you gave it away only so that people would call you charitable."

Then the Lord of Power will summon all those who sacrificed their lives in Holy Wars. He will ask them, "And how did you spend your life?"

They will reply, "We gave away our life in your Way."

The Lord of Power and the angels will laugh and call them liars and say, "You sacrificed your lives only so people could call you courageous and dub you martyrs."

—Ghazali

THE BRIDE-SOUL LONGS FOR HER HUSBAND, THE BELOVED

When will that day dawn, Mother,
When the One I took birth for
Holds me to His heart with deathless love?
I long for the bliss of divine union.
I long to lose my body, mind, and soul
And become one with my husband.
When will that day dawn, Mother?
Husband, fulfill now the longing I have had
Since before the universe was made.
Enter me completely and release me.
In terrible lonely years without You
I yearn and yearn for You.
I spend sleepless nights hunting for You,
Gazing into darkness after You,
With unblinking hopeless eyes.
When will that day dawn, Mother?
When will my Lord hold me to His heart?
My empty bed, like a hungry tigress,
Devours me whenever I try to sleep.
Listen to your slave's prayer —
Come and put out this blaze of agony
That consumes my soul and body.
When will He hold me to His heart?
When will that day dawn, Mother?

Kabir sings, "If I ever meet You, my Beloved,
I'll cling to you so fiercely You melt into me;
I'll sing from inside You songs of union,
World-dissolving songs of Eternal Bliss."

—Kabir

THE TRAIN OF THE BELOVED'S DRESS

A dervish appeared among one of the Bedouin tribes. A young man offered him a meal. While the young man was serving the dervish, he fell down and fainted. The dervish asked the others who were there why he had fainted and they said, "He has fallen passionately in love with his cousin. While she was moving in her tent, the young man glimpsed the dust raised by the train of her dress and fainted."

The dervish went to the girl's tent and said, "I would like to intercede for the young man. Show him your favor! His love for you is so great!"

The girl smiled. "He cannot stand glimpsing even the train of my dress. How do you imagine he could live in my presence?"

—Sadi

In the Dust

Don't be amazed at those murdered
In the dust at the Friend's door.
Be amazed at how anyone can survive
With soul intact!

—Tohfah of Syria

The Lord Is in Me

The Lord is in me, and the Lord is in you,
As life is hidden in every seed.
So rubble your pride, my friend,
And look for Him within you.

When I sit in the heart of His world
A million suns blaze with light,
A burning blue sea spreads across the sky,
Life's turmoil falls quiet,
All the stains of suffering wash away.

Listen to the unstruck bells and drums!
Love is here; plunge into its rapture!
Rains pour down without water;
Rivers are streams of light.

How could I ever express
How blessed I feel
To revel in such vast ecstasy
In my own body?

This is the music
Of soul and soul meeting,
Of the forgetting of all grief.
This is the music
That transcends all coming and going.

—Kabir

TRUE REMEMBRANCE

True remembrance is that you contemplate the remembrance of yourself by Him-who-is-remembered, while you never cease remembering Him. Then your remembrance of Him will be annihilated in His remembrance of you, and only His remembrance of you will remain and continue, beyond time and space.

—Fatimah Barda'iyah

MY GOD AND MY LORD

Eyes are at rest, the stars are setting.
Hushed are the stirrings of birds in their nests,
Of monsters in the ocean.

You are the Just who knows no change,
The Balance that can never swerve,
The Eternal which never passes away.

The doors of Kings are bolted now and guarded by soldiers.
Your Door is open to all who call upon You.

My Lord,
Each love is now alone with his beloved.
And I am alone with You.

— Rabia

I FOLLOW THE RELIGION OF LOVE

My heart has become capable of every form:
It is a pasture for gazelles,
And a monastery for Christian monks,
And a temple for idols,
And the Ka'aba of the pilgrims,

And the tablets of the Torah,
And the book of the Koran.
I follow the religion of Love:
Whatever path Love's camel takes,
That is my religion and my faith.

—Ibn Arabi

LET ME BE MAD

O Incomparable Giver of life, cut reason loose at last!
Let it wander grey-eyed from vanity to vanity.
Shatter open my skull, pour in it the wine of madness!
Let me be mad, as You; mad with You, with us.
Beyond the sanity of fools is a burning desert
Where Your sun is whirling in every atom:
Beloved, drag me there, let me roast in Perfection!

—Rumi

I AM NOT TO BLAME

If heaven rings with my cries, I am not to blame

Nor if deserts glitter with my tears . . .
You are my soul — I run after you —
Who could blame me for chasing my soul?

—Rumi

Your Madness Is the Diamond

The universe contemplates nothing but Your Face.
When they see You, souls weep and tear off their skins.
In the eyes of those whom passion has made wise,
Your madness is the diamond, the Fountain of Paradise.

—Rumi

No End

One day, I met an old woman on a beach who revealed to me many mysteries of the Path. I asked her, "What is the end of love?"
She laughed, "You fool, love has no end."
I asked her, "Why?"
And she replied, "Because the Beloved has no end."

—Dhu al-Nun

◆

PART IV

Ordeal and Annihilation

ORDEAL
AND ANNIHILATION

✦

The Sufis say that the quest is composed of two different but related journeys—the journey *to* God and the journey *in* God. The journey to God is one that the soul makes as it leaves the world and all the games of the false self behind in a progressive blaze of love and gnosis. This journey ends—with the grace of God—in Union, in a permanent possession of conscious divine identity. The second journey begins with Union and ends nowhere, for it is taken in love as Love, and Love is infinite. For the journey to God to become the journey in God and for the seeker to be permanently established in divine consciousness, a death has to happen—the death of the false self.

Even the most impassioned mystic lover of the Beloved is still conscious of the "self that loves" (and is loved); however irradiated by passion and the illuminations of direct gnosis, the seeker's "self" still remains intact. But the culmination of the work of Love is that the seeker is at last given the strength to allow himself to be utterly destroyed by Love, to have his being wiped out and annihilated in Love so it can be re-made in it. This "death" is known in all serious mystical traditions; in the Christian tradition, it is called the Dark Night of the Soul. The Sufis, like St. John of the Cross and Angela of Foligno, know that no one can live the Resurrected Life without having passed through all the strippings, humiliations, and torments of the Crucifixion.

The test of the Cross of Annihilation is the supreme test of the seeker's sincerity, and only someone who has prepared himself for a long time (and been prepared by God) can possibly go through it. In one sense, the whole of the quest up to this stage has been a preparation for this great death. The secret goal of all of Love's gifts, ecstasies, and visions is to give the seeker the strength and fathomless trust necessary to accept the final death that is annihilation. Only a seeker who has opened his or her whole being to the glory of Love will find in themselves the mad abandon necessary to die into Love and be reborn as One with it.

One of the greatest gifts to us all from the Sufi mystics is their wisdom about suffering and ordeal. They can teach us not only about the necessity of repeated ordeal to the drastic purification of the being, but also how to suffer with increasing trust, and even gratitude, those trials that are sent by Love to help us die into eternal life. What gradually becomes clear to the seeker as he subjects himself to the alchemy of love is that "dying" and "birth" into Love are two halves, two sides of one miraculous process. Learning how to "die" to the false self—often in atrocious suffering—is simultaneously learning how to come alive in a fresh and expanded dimension of Truth. Such knowledge has to be practiced in a thousand small terrors and losses before the final horror and final loss of annihilation can even be approached, let alone endured.

At exactly the appointed moment, the trial of the Cross arrives—tailored to the personality of each seeker: precisely the right catastrophe or set of catastrophes are prepared by the grace of the Beloved to help the seeker abandon even the most vestigial trust in his own powers and give himself wholly over to the darkness of God.

In this abandonment to the darkness of God, the false self is crucified and the true self born forever, never again to die in any world or dimension.

THE ROSE

Misery and joy have the same shape in this world:
You may call the rose an open heart or a broken heart.

—Dard

NO GUTS, NO GLORY

Nasrudin addressed a large crowd and shouted, "Do you want knowledge without ordeal, truth without lies, attainment without any hard work, and progress without sacrifice?"

Everyone yelled "Yes!"

"Marvelous!" said Nasrudin. "I do also, and if I ever find out how to manage it, I'll be thrilled to let you know."

—Nasrudin

WHO CAN CURE MY SICKNESS?

Who can cure my sickness? I have become an outcast. Where are family and home? No path leads back to them and none to my Beloved. My name and reputation are both shattered, like glass smashed on rock; the drum that once beat out good news is broken and now all my ears hear is the harsh drumbeat of separation.

I follow my Beloved obediently; she owns my soul. If she orders me, "Get drunk!" I do; if she tells me to be mad, I am.

—Majnun in Nizami's *Leyla and Majnun*

HOW COULD I NOT ACKNOWLEDGE HIM?

A Bedouin was asked, "Do you acknowledge the Lord?"

He replied, "How could I not acknowledge Him who has sent me hunger, made me naked and poor, and driven me to wander from country to country?"

As he spoke those words, he entered a state of ecstasy.

—Abu Said Ibn Abi Khayr

HE KNOWS

He knows all our good and all our evil.
Nothing is, or can be, hidden from Him.
He knows too what the best medicine is
To cure our pain
And rescue the destroyed.
Be humble, for He exalts the humble.

—Sheikh Ansari

✦

O MY GOD AND MY CREATOR

O my God and my Creator,
Although You afflict me
With torments of every kind,
It is nothing in comparison
With being far from You!
And though You bless me
With all the wealth of heaven,
It would still be less than the ecstasy
Your love has showered on my heart.

—Roqiyah

TRUE GLORY

It is glorious for a person to bear the burden of trouble imposed upon him by the Beloved; in reality, misfortune is glory, and prosperity humiliation. Glory is that which makes you present with God, and humiliation is that which makes you absent from Him.

—Mahjub

◆

TELL MY CRUEL ONE HOW I SUFFER

Yesterday, I sent You a star as a messenger.
I told him, "Take my greetings to my Moon of Beauty!"
I prostrated myself: "Take this prostration to My Sun,
To Him, by whose radiance, stones are turned to gold!"
I opened my heart and showed him its wounds
And told him, "Tell my cruel One how I suffer!"
I stumbled up and down until my heart, that child, grew calm;
A child falls asleep if you rock its cradle.
Beloved, each second You heal a thousand wrecks like me!
From the beginning, the Kingdom of Union with You
Was always and forever the true home of my being:
How long will you leave in exile my tortured heart?

—Rumi

A FLAME KEEPS LEAPING IN MY HEART

I have not only lost you; I no longer know myself. Who am I?
I keep turning and turning around myself, asking, "What is your
name? Are you in love? With whom? Are you loved? By whom?"
A flame keeps leaping in my heat, a vast, immeasurable flame
which has charred my entire being to ashes. Do I still know where
I live? Can I still taste what I eat? I am lost in my own desert . . .
I am pulled towards death; death lives within me.

—Majnun in Nizami's *Leyla and Majnun*

DO NOT BLAME LOVE

Do not blame Love for the agony it brings;
Love is the King of all paths,
And the heart not wild with longing
Is already dead, already a burial ground.

—Kabir

SUFFERING AND THE INFINITE TREASURE

No one has ever attained by suffering
The Infinite Treasure of Union —
Yet, strangely, without suffering
No one ever saw that Treasure.

—Abu Said

✦

THE PROCESS OF FIRE

When does gold ore become gold? When it is put through a process of fire. So the human being during the training becomes as pure as gold through suffering. It is the burning away of the dross. Suffering has great redeeming quality. As a drop of water falling in the desert sand is sucked up immediately, so we must become nothing and nowhere . . . and disappear.

—Bhai Sahib

THE ROBE OF HONOR

Whatever the blow that arrives from heaven,
Wait to receive a robe of honor afterwards:
He is not a King who thrashes you and then
Does not give you a crown and a throne to rest on.
The world is worth less than the eye of a mosquito,
Yet for a single blow there is infinite reward:
Take from your neck now the world's gold collar,
Receive with no protection the blows God sends.
Didn't the Prophets receive blows on their necks?
That pain is what forced them to hold their heads high.
Never abandon your innermost core even a moment
So the Beloved will always find you at home.
Otherwise, He'll remove His robe of honor and say,
"I came to see him Myself, and found no one in."

—Rumi

✦

TRUE KNOWLEDGE

This, I've discovered, is true knowledge—
Those who scramble to get into a boat
Sink like a stone midstream,
While the shelterless and abandoned

Reach the other shore.
Those who dare to take
The hard, winding, thorny road
Get to town in the end;
Those who stroll the easy highway
Get robbed or even killed
Soon after they set out.
Everyone's wound in illusion's web —
The so-called "holy" as much as the worldly,
And those who run for safety
Under the comforting dais
Of form and ritual and dogma —
Well, life's hurricane lashes them.
Stay out in the open:
You'll be left safe and dry.
The ones Love never savages
Live in boredom and pain;
Those Love devours like a cannibal
Live in bliss forever.
The ones who lose their own eyes
Come to see the whole Creation
Blazing in their own Light;
Those who hold on to their sight
Remain blind as bats in full noon.
When I began to awake to Truth
I saw how bizarre and crazy the world really is!

—Kabir

THE LAST VEIL

The final goal of love is to become bare as a desert. As long as love is in the initial stage of its journey, the form of the Beloved provides the inner food needed by the lover. Once love has reached its final goal, however, it leaves all form far behind.

Just before this ultimate station is reached, the form of the Beloved appears in all its perfection and falls as an obstacle between the lover and love. All possible effort must be expended to remove this last veil.

—Ghazali

THE STORY OF A RAINDROP

A raindrop fell from a spring cloud, saw the vastness of the sea for the first time, and was astounded and ashamed.

"What am I next to the sea?" it whispered to itself. "Compared to the sea I am less than nothing, I am as if I didn't exist at all."

Moved by the raindrop's self-contempt, an oyster took it into its heart and Fate so shaped its destiny that eventually the raindrop became a famous royal pearl. It was raised up because it was humble. It knocked at the door of Annihilation and became at last alive.

—Sadi

DIE OF SURRENDER

Die of surrender, you will live forever.
Be put to death through surrender —
Death will no longer exist for you —
You will have died already.

— Traditional Persian poem

✦

SUFFERINGS ARE WINGS

A man who does not know mystical suffering
is not really alive —
He is like ice.
Suffering in the soul is a sign of life;
It shows submission to God.

The body lives by the soul;
The soul lives by this holy suffering.
He who is deprived of it
Cannot be called a human being.

A pregnant woman never gives birth without pain.
An army never conquers without difficulties.
Union without suffering is impossible —
A cold heart never comes anywhere near it.

114

Sufferings are wings for the bird of the soul;
A bird without wings cannot take flight.
So weep and groan and lament, my friend,
So you can free yourself from this prison
And fly to that placeless place where you will be
Free forever in the boundless sky of God.

—Sultan Valad

✦

THE SUN MUST COME

Since Love has made ruins of my heart
The sun must come and illumine them.
Such generosity has broken me with shame:
The King prayed for me, and granted me His prayer.
How many times, just to calm me, did He show His Face?
I said, "I saw His Face," but it was only a veil.
He charred a universe through the flaming-out of this veil.
O my God! How could such a King ever be unveiled?
Love reared in front of me, and I followed Him.
He turned and seized me like an eagle—
What a blessing it was to be His prey!
I plunged into a sea of ecstasy, and fled all pain.
If anguish is not delicious meat for you,

115

It is because you have never tasted this wine.
The Prophets accept all agony and trust it
For the Water has never feared the Fire.

—Rumi

STORY OF A VULTURE AND A KITE

A vulture said to a kite, "No one can see as far as I."

"That may be true," said the kite. "But what exactly do you see as you stare down at the desert?"

The vulture cried, "I see a grain of wheat."

They flew to the ground. The vulture settled on the grain of wheat and was immediately caught in a trap. How could he know that Fate had plans to ensnare him?

Not every oyster shelters a pearl and not every archer hits the target.

The kite said, "What use was it to see the grain when you could not see that it was part of your enemy's game?"

The trapped vulture said, "Caution doesn't help with destiny."

When the decrees of Eternity are called into action, the sharpest eyes are blinded by Fate.

Out in the ocean, there is no shoreline and the swimmer sweats in vain.

—Sadi

EVEN IF YOU LOSE ALL YOU HAVE

Learn the meaning of that secret
That God revealed in the Koran:
Whether He makes you happy or unhappy,
Whether He makes you sad or gives you hope,
Even if you lose all you have
Or suffer extremely in the spirit,
Be patient: a hundred divine graces
Are coming from His hand to you.

He who endures patiently the pain
That is sent from God
Will, it is certain, obtain
The strength and truth of faith.
Marvelous news is sent to the patient;
They will win a great joy.

You must be able to perceive grace
Even when His divine anger lashes you,
And think of Him always with serenity,
And always, whatever happens, cling to Him
With all your heart and all your soul.

—Sultan Valad

A PIECE OF WAX, A NEEDLE, AND A HAIR

On one occasion, Rabia sent three things to Hasan: a piece of wax, a needle, and a hair.

"Light up the world," she told him, "although like wax you burn yourself. And, like a needle, be always busy in spiritual work, while outwardly barren. When you acquire these virtues, make your ego thin as a hair, so all your efforts are not wasted."

—Rabia

✦

ONE LOVE

One day Rayhanah went to see Hayyunah. That night there was a wild rainstorm and Rayhanah was terrified. Hayyunah, however, laughed and scolded her and said, "You tremble! If I were ever to feel that my heart holds any love besides Him or any fear of anything other than Him, I would strike it with a knife!"

—Attar

THE STANDING OF THE SEA

He stood me in the sea.
I saw the ships sinking and the planks floating;
I saw the planks sinking.
He said to me,
"No one on board will be saved."

Danger for one who throws himself in and does not come on board.

Destruction for those who come on board and do not accept danger.

He said, "In danger there is a part of salvation."
Then the wave came
And swept up what was beneath it
And raced along the shore.

He said to me:

The surface of the sea is an unattainable brilliance,
The depth of the sea is an unfathomable darkness,
And what is between them? Sea monsters who give no refuge. . . .

Do not sail on the sea, or the ship will veil you.
Do not throw yourself in, or the sea itself will veil you.

In the sea there are precipices. Which will hold you up?

When you give yourself to the sea and drown,
You become like one of its creatures.

I would cheat you if I led you to an other-than-me.

If you die in an other-than-me,
You belong to that in which you die.

This world belongs to the one I have turned from it
And from whom I have turned away the world.

The world to come belongs to the one I turn it to —
To whoever turns to me.

— Niffari

◆

Do Not Fight against God's Will

I went with Sofyan Thawri to pay Rabia a visit while she was sick. Her presence so overwhelmed us with awe, however, that neither of us could say a word.

"Say something," I said to Sofyan at last.

"Why don't you ask God to lighten your pain?" he asked Rabia.

"He Himself wills that I suffer, isn't that evident to you?" she replied.

"Yes," I said.

"You say 'yes,'" Rabia went on, "but you still urge me to pursue my own desire against His, although it is wrong to fight against the Beloved's will."

— Abdul Wahed Ebn Aer

WHY SO RESTLESS, SO IMPATIENT, MY HEART?

Why so restless, so impatient, my heart?
He watches over birds, animals, the tiniest insect —
He loved you even when you were in your mother's belly.
Do you seriously imagine
He will not look after you
Now that you are here?

O my heart, how could you bear
To turn from His smile
And stray so far from Him?

You have abandoned your true Beloved
And are hankering after others —
This is why all your works are useless.

—Kabir

THE REAL WORK

Hasan of Basra was given to extreme ascetic practices. Through these, he won certain occult powers which he took great pride in flaunting.

One day he saw Rabia on the bank of the river. He threw his prayer rug onto the water and shouted to her, "Rabia, come! Let's pray together!"

Rabia replied, "Is it really necessary for you to sell yourself like this? If it is, it is because you are weak."

Then, Rabia ascended into the air on her prayer rug and called down, "Hasan, come up here! Everyone will see us!" Hasan, who was not as advanced as she, stayed silent.

Rabia said to him, "What you did a fish can do. What I did a fly can do. The real work is beyond either of our tricks. The only thing necessary is to do the real work."

—Rabia

✦

FRESH SKIN

It has been said, "The moment is a sword." Just as a sword cuts, so the moment prevails in what the Real makes happen and completes. It is said, "The sword is gentle to touch, and whoever handles it gently is not harmed by it. Whoever handles it roughly is cut." The same goes for the moment; whoever submits to its command is saved, and whoever fights against it is toppled and destroyed.

I heard my teacher Abu Ali al-Daqqaq say, "The moment is a file. It wears you down without rubbing you out. If it were to rub you out, you would be liberated. However, the moment robs you without entirely annihilating you." He used to recite:

Every day that passes
Robs me of part of me,
Leaves my heart a fresh part of loss
And passes away.

He also recited:

I am just like those in hell-fire:
Their skin is roasted to a crisp
But they go on making for misery
Fresh skin.

—Qushayri

✦

ON SINCERITY

Hasan Basri, Malik Dinar, and Shaqiq Balkhi went to see Rabia. They talked about sincerity.

Hasan said, "The sincere person is patient under his Lord's blows."

Rabia said, "That reeks of egoism."

Shaqiq said, "The sincere person is the one who rejoices in the Lord's blows."

Rabia laughed, "Surely you can do better than that!"

The three of them said, "Well, Rabia, you speak now."

Rabia said, "The sincere person forgets the wound of any blow in the vision of his Lord. Why should this strike anyone as absurd? Didn't the Egyptian women forget they were cutting their own hands as they gazed, stupefied, at Joseph's beauty?"

—Rabia

THE HARDEST ACT OF PATIENCE

A man came before Shebli and said to him, "What is the hardest act of patience for someone who is patient?"

Shebli said, "Patience in God."

"No," said the man.

Shebli said, "Patience for God."

The man said, "No."

Shebli said, "Patience with God."

"No."

Shebli grew furious and said, "Well, damn you, what do you think?"

The man said, "Patience without God."

Shebli let out a scream that nearly tore apart his spirit.

—Sarraj

THE WAY OF THE HOLY ONES

Don't speak of your suffering — He is speaking.
Don't look for Him everywhere — He's looking for you.

An ant's foot touches a leaf, He senses it;
A pebble shifts in a streambed, He knows it.

If there's a worm hidden deep in a rock,
He'll know its body, tinier than an atom,

The sound of its praise, its secret ecstasy —
All this He knows by divine knowing.

He has given the tiniest worm its food;
He has opened to you the Way of the Holy Ones.

— Sanai

RABIA AND THE DONKEY

Rabia decided to make the pilgrimage to Mecca and set off into the desert. She took with her a donkey, which she loaded with her few belongings. In the middle of the desert, however, the donkey died. The others in her caravan said, "We'll carry your things for you."

Rabia replied, "I have not come this far by putting my faith and trust in you. You go on ahead."

So the caravan went on without her. Rabia cried out "O my Lord, do real kings treat a helpless woman in this fashion? You invited me to your house. Then You went and killed my donkey in the middle of my journey and abandoned me alone in the desert."

Immediately, the donkey got up. Rabia loaded it again and continued on her pilgrimage. The person who told this story said that a little while later he saw that little donkey being sold.

— Rabia

HELPLESS IN THE DESERT

While Rabia was on her pilgrimage to Mecca, she was abandoned in the desert. She cried out, "O my Lord, I am in torment. Where will I go now? I am just a clump of earth and the House I am going to is a rock. I must possess You."

Then the Ultimate Real One spoke to her in her heart without any veil, "O Rabia, you wash in the blood of eighteen thousand worlds! Don't you understand that when Moses (Peace be always with him!) hungered for a vision, we threw a few atoms of Self-manifestation upon Sinai and it shattered into forty pieces!"

— Rabia

BLESSINGS IN DISGUISE

One day, Nasrudin was sitting drinking tea with a group of seekers. One of them (who believed he knew everything) stood up and said, "My master taught me that humanity can never evolve as it must until the person who has not been wronged is as indignant about a wrong as the one who has been."

The group gasped with admiration at what they thought to be the profundity of this statement. Then Nasrudin said, "My master taught me that no one should become angry about anything until he is sure that what he believes to be a wrong *is* one — and not a blessing in disguise!"

— Nasrudin

THE ONE YOU KILL

The one You kill,
Lord,
Does not smell of blood,
And the one You burn
Does not reek of smoke.

He You burn laughs as he burns
And the one You kill,
As You kill him,
Cries out in ecstasy.

—Sheikh Ansari

✦

THE NOOSE

When al-Hallaj was put in prison
For saying he was one with God,
Shebli, his friend, asked him,
"What is the love you speak of?"

"Come tomorrow and I'll tell you,"
Al-Hallaj answered.
Tomorrow came and Shebli found him
In front of the gallows.

Al-Hallaj looked at him and said,
"Now you can see the answer:
Love begins by alluring the 'I'
And ends like this:

"Its noose gets tighter and tighter
To squeeze out the self.

Then comes the test of the Cross.
Stay if you understand; if you don't, leave now."

—Sheikh Ansari

CHECKMATE

The King of Love has you in checkmate.
Do not be angry, do not look for revenge.
Enter into Annihilation's garden and contemplate
The paradise that lives in your eternal soul.
When you have detached yourself from yourself,
Your gaze will penetrate beyond the heavens.
When the Emperor of hidden meanings arrives,
Do not demand of Him miracles or wonders
For miracles and wonders are only signs.
The shore of the Ocean is visible for a while
But when it is flooded, what then remains?
Shams of Tabriz, your glory has conquered us;
We are your slaves; accept our amazed cries.

—Rumi

FANA: ANNIHILATION

When God, the One and Only and the all-victorious, unveils Himself to one of his servants in His quality of the destroyer, then that servant sees everything annihilated. Then, "everything is annihilated except His face." As the Koran says, "Everything on the earth will be annihilated and there will remain only the Face of Your Lord who is at once terrible in majesty and generous."

It is essential to die before death to know this state. This death has to take place through a willed and resolute choice and that person in whom this state of death appears will see the total annihilation of everything except God and will no longer exist himself. This non-existence is total non-existence. This state is known as "Annihilation-in-God"; nothing remains in it but the divine splendor.

Anyone who comes to know this state is destroyed and made nothing. Yet, God also streams him an existence from the heart of His own existence and adorns him with divine color. All qualities inside him and outside him are transformed. On that day, earth becomes another earth altogether, and heaven another heaven.

Then, God Himself gives the person who knows this state a divine sight, ear, and tongue. His servant passes through non-existence by the existence of God Himself.

His real understanding and knowledge begins after this.

—Ibn Arabi

THE UTTERLY BURNT ONE

When your heart is consumed with longing and burned to ashes, the breeze of Love arises and sweeps up the ashes, and fills heaven and earth with the utterly burnt one.

—Kharaqani

THE TWO BEWILDERMENTS

Dhu al-Nun was asked, "What is the first step the gnostic must overcome?"

He replied, "Bewilderment, then need, then union, then bewilderment again."

The first bewilderment is at God's acts and gifts towards him; for he sees that his gratitude can never be adequate to God's gifts, and he knows that he is required to be grateful for them. He knows too that, even if he is grateful, that gratitude itself is a gift from God for which he should be grateful.

The second bewilderment is in the trackless desert of unification, in which the gnostic's understanding is utterly lost, and his intellect shrinks before the greatness of God's power and awe and majesty. This second bewilderment releases a man from all pride, because it teaches him he can never know anything. He wanders in desert after desert, glory after glory.

—Kalabadhi

THE TAVERN HAUNTERS

Being a tavern haunter means
Being sprung free of yourself.

The tavern is where lovers tryst,
Where the bird of the soul comes to rest
In a sanctuary beyond space and time.
The tavern haunter wanders lonely in a desert
And sees the whole world as a mirage.
This desert is limitless and endless —
No one has seen its beginning or its end,
And even if you wandered in it a hundred years
You would not find yourself, or anyone else.
Those who live there have no feet or heads,
Are neither "believers" nor "unbelievers."
Drunk on the wine of selflessness,
They have given up good and evil alike.
Drunk, without lips or mouth, on Truth
They have thrown away all thoughts of name and fame,
All talk of wonders, visions, spiritual states,
Dreams, secret rooms, lights, miracles.

The aroma of the Divine Wine
Has made them abandon everything;
The taste for Annihilation
Has sent them all sprawling like drunkards.
For one sip of the wine of ecstasy,

They have thrown away pilgrim staff, water jar, and rosary.
They fall, and then they rise again,
Sometimes bright in union,
Sometimes lost in the pain of separation;
Now pouring tears of blood,
Now raised to a world of bliss,
Stretching out their necks like racers;
Now, with blackened faces, staring at a wall,
Or faces reddened with Unity, chained to a gibbet;
Now whirling in mystic dance,
Lost in the arms of the Beloved,
Losing head and foot like the revolving heavens.
Every passage that the Singer sings them
Transmits the rapture of the invisible world,
For mystic singing is not only words and sounds;
Each note unveils a priceless mystery.

They have thrown away their senses
And run from all color and perfume,
And washed in purified wine
All the different dyes: black, green, or blue.
To them, devotion and piety are only hypocrisy;
They are weary of being either masters or disciples;
They have swept the dust of dunghills from their souls,
Without telling even a tiny part of what they see,

And grasped in bliss at the swirling robes of drunkards.
They have drunk one cup of the pure wine
And have become—at last, at long last—real Sufis.

—Shabistari

ONLY GOD

In the marketplace, in the monastery, I saw only God.
In the valley, on the mountaintop, I saw only God.

In the darkness of ordeal I saw Him bright beside me.
In good luck or tragedy, I saw only God.

In prayer, in fasting, in celebration, in contemplation,
In all the glory of the Prophet's religion, I saw only God.

I did not see "soul" or "body," "accident" or "substance."
I did not see "attributes" or "causes," I saw only God.

I opened wide my eyes and by the blaze of His Face
Everything was lit with vision, and I saw only God.

In the fire of His ecstasy I melted like a candle;
His flames rushed at me from all sides, and I saw only God.

When I looked with my own eyes I saw only myself.

When I came to look with God's eyes, I saw only God.

I was annihilated by Love and vanished into Nowhere —
Suddenly, I was the All-living One, and saw only God.

—Baba Kuhi of Shiraz

❖

PART V

*The Life of
Union*

The Life of Union

Bayazid, a ninth-century Sufi master, once said, "I sloughed off my self as a snake sloughs off its skin. And I looked into myself and saw that I am Him."

In the "Life of Union"—what the Sufis call *Baqa* or "subsistence in Eternal being"—that "seeing that I am Him" is continual and normal.

The ultimate perfection in Sufism—as in all the most serious mystical traditions—is not one of perpetual trance or continued ecstatic vision. Those marvelous fervors and revelations belong to the penultimate stages of the Path; Union itself is characterized by effortlessness, joy, peace, and a buoyant unflappable sobriety of being. In the life of Union, lover and Beloved are consciously and normally One. This ultimate stage is not usually one of extreme ecstasies or revelations; the Self now lives a human divine life, conscious at all moments of its divine origin and immortal consciousness.

As in all the mature mystical traditions, the aim of the quest for the Sufi is not to live in a trance of bliss in God, but to live as

139

a part of God on earth and in time, loving and serving all beings with some small power of God's selfless humility.

Many of the greatest Sufi masters have not been recluses or hermits, but tailors or potters or small town businessmen, men and women, who live their supreme realization realistically and humbly at the center of ordinary life. As Abu Sa'id wrote in the eighth century, "The perfect mystic is not an ecstatic devotee lost in contemplation of Oneness, nor a saintly recluse shunning all commerce with mankind; but the true saint goes in and out amongst the people and eats and sleeps with them and buys and sells in the market and takes part in social intercourse and never forgets God for a single moment."

Such "true saints" become to Love what a hand is to a person; they become efficient instruments in Reality of the will of God, servants of God and servants of all beings in and for God. Wherever they are, a light of God is; whatever they do, God does in them; their words inspire divine love and their actions radiate the clarity of divine justice and the generosity of divine mercy. What is remarkable about those who reach this glory is that they are always humble and integrated. As Junayd said of the realized Sufi, "She is one whose heart keeps pace with her foot. She is entirely present; her soul is where her body is, and her body where her soul is, and her soul where her foot is."

Those who live the Life of Union pray with each breath the prayer of Sheikh Ansari:

Give me life
So I can spend it
Working for the salvation of the world.

Fana and Baqa

Fana (the loss of self in God) and *Baqa* (remaining in communion with God in the midst of worldly activity) are two terms that apply to the servant who acknowledges that God is One. The first level of meaning of Fana and Baqa is the passing away of ignorance into the enduring condition of knowledge; the passing away of revolt into an enduring state of obedience; the passing away of coldheartedness into the state of continual adoration; and the passing away of the examination of the servant's actions, which are temporary, into the direct vision of the Divine Grace, which is eternal.

— Sarraj

In the Desert of No Attributes

The people of perfection have realized all stations and states and gone beyond these to the station above both Majesty and Beauty; they have no attributes and no description.

Someone asked Bayazid, "How are you this morning?"

He replied, "I have no morning and no evening; morning and evening belong to someone whom attributes limit, and I have no attributes."

— Ibn Arabi

LOVE OCCUPIES AND ADORNS MY HOUSE

Who do you think I am? A drunkard? A love-addled idiot, a slave of my senses, made senseless by desire? Understand—I have soared far above such things; I am the King of Love in majesty. My soul is purified from the night of lust, my longing is purified of all shadowy hungers, my mind is free from all shame. I have shattered the teeming bazaar of the senses in my body.

Love is the essence of my being. Love is fire and I am wood charred by the flame. Love occupies and adorns my house; my self tied up its bundle and vanished. You imagine that you see me, but I no longer exist; what remains is the Beloved. . . .

—Majnun in Nizami's *Leyla and Majnun*

BE FREE LIKE THE CYPRESS

They asked a philosopher, "What secret is there in this, that while God Most High has created so many famous trees, and made them fruitful, people do not term any one of them 'free' except the cypress?"

He replied, "Every other tree has fruit at an appointed time: at one time, during the right season, it is fresh and green; at another, it is withered; but the cypress is always blooming and fresh, and such is the state of the free."

—Sadi

THE EPIPHANY OF ESSENCE

The persistence-in-God which comes to perfect beings signifies that the seeker of Truth arrives, after his annihilation, at the epiphany of Essence which leads him to the state of super-existence: he sees himself then in the Absolute, without any more material, corporal, or spiritual individuality; he establishes that his consciousness embraces everything that the entire universe contains, all the divine attributes, and that he sees nothing but one single Reality. This is the true Divine Unity. As Shabistari wrote:

> Bayazid, who cried out, "Glory to me!" at that very moment
> Entered the Kingdom of these sublime truths.
> For that very reason, that Ocean of Purity said,
> "There is nothing under my robe but God."
> Al-Hallaj, who announced, "I am the Supreme Reality,"
> Understood also the same final truth
> That was taken, alas, for blasphemous pretension.
> Mohammed, who proclaimed, "There is nothing in the two worlds but God,"
> Also was right and spoke from total knowledge.
> If not a single trace of individuality remains in you,
> You will understand what I have just expressed.

> —Lahiji

The Clarity of Sobriety

Totally present in God, he is totally lost to self. And so he is present before God, absent in himself—absent and present at the same time. He is where he is not, and he is not where he is. After he has not been, he is where he is before the Creation began. He is himself, after not being himself. He is existent in himself and existent in God after being existent in God and non-existent in himself. This is because he has gone beyond the drunkenness of God's overwhelming and come to the clarity of sobriety, where contemplation is restored to him once more; by its light, he can put all things in their true place and assess all things justly.

—Junayd

Whoever Draws Near

Whoever loves God will win His friendship.
Whoever becomes joyful will fill with desire.
Whoever is full of desire will become bewildered.
Whoever becomes bewildered will become brave.
Whoever becomes brave will reach Him.
Whoever reaches Him will enter into Union.
Whoever enters into Union will become a Knower.
Whoever becomes a Knower will be drawn near.

Whoever draws near will never fall asleep
And the rays of sublime heartbreak will engulf him.

—Hayyunah

LOVE'S HURRICANE

Love's hurricane has come!
The whirlwind of Knowledge has arrived!
My thatched roof of Delusion
Has been flung to the four directions!
My hut of Illusion
So carefully crafted
Has come careening down!
Its two posts of duality
have crashed to the ground!
Its rafters of desire
have been split by lightning!
Thunderbolts have collapsed
All its eaves of greed!
Its big stone jar of evil habits
Has smashed in a million pieces!

With contemplation and clear devotion,
The Holy Ones have rebuilt my roof.

It is strong and unmoving now
And never leaks or drips.

When lies and all deceit
Ran out of my body's house,
I realized the Lord
In all His splendor.
Rain came down in torrents.

After the wild storm,
Torrents of divine love
Drenched me, body and soul.
Then, O Kabir, the sun soared out,
The Sun of Glory, the Sun of Realization,
And darkness dissolved forever.

—Kabir

WHEN I LOVE A SERVANT

The true Sufi becomes humbler every hour, for every hour takes him closer to God. True Sufis see without knowledge, without sight, without receiving any information, without observation, without description, without being veiled, without a veil. They are not themselves. If they can be said to exist at all, they exist in God. Every movement of theirs is caused by God; their words are God's words spoken with their tongues; their sight is God's, who has entered into their eyes. God the Glorious has said, "When I love a servant, I, the Lord, am his ear so he hears by Me; I am his eye so he sees by Me; I am his tongue so he speaks by Me; I am his hand so he grasps by Me."

—Dhu al-Nun

No Trace or Sign

Bayazid said, "The first time I went into the Holy House I saw the Holy House. The second time, I saw the Lord of the House. The third, I saw neither the House nor its Lord."

Bayazid meant by this, "I became lost in God, so I knew nothing. If I had seen anything at all, I would have been God." An anecdote bears out this interpretation: A man came to the door of Bayazid and called out.

"Who are you looking for?" Bayazid asked.

"Bayazid," the man replied.

"You poor fool!" Bayazid said. "I have been looking for Bayazid for thirty years, and cannot find any trace or sign of him."

—Bayazid Bistami

THE STORY OF LOVE

The story of Love can never be told.
It is the sherbet of the dumb man
Who eats it and smiles silently.

Without any earth and without any seed,
The tree of Divine Love just grows and grows,
Heavy with a million radiant fruits
My Lover picks for me to taste.
The story of Love can never be told.

When I calmed my mind
And entered my heart,
The Love of the Lord
Leapt like a flame within me.
All my old ideas and beliefs
Just blew away like chaff in the wind.

It wasn't because of anything I am;
It wasn't because of anything I did;
But only because of Him and His wild, miraculous, grace
That I learned at long last the lesson of Love.
My coming and going have ended;
My mind has melted in the Mind.

Don't ask me to speak any more —
The story of Love can never be told.

—Kabir

Wadatja!

Bistami said, "Renunciation has no station."

I asked, "Why?"

He said, "Because I spent three days in renunciation. When the fourth day arrived, I left it behind me. The first day I renounced this world and all it contains. The second day I renounced the next world and all that it contains. The third day, I renounced everything other than God. When the fourth day arrived, there was nothing left for me other than God. I understood.

"I heard a voice saying, 'Abu Yazid, you will not be able to bear being with Us.'

"I said, 'But this is what I want!'

"Then I heard the voice say, *'Wadatja!* You've found what you were looking for!'"

—Sulami

Tawakkul (Confidence in God)

When the seeker understands that all is in God and there is no other force but His, he acquires stability. He realizes that the powers he thought were his belong, in reality, to God; that he is only a locus of the divine manifestation and a receptacle. Like the prophet Abraham, he attains the station of *tawakkul* (confidence in God) and understands that everything that happens comes from God.

As Abraham says in the Koran, "It is He who directs me; He who feeds me and gives me to drink; it is He who heals me when I am sick; He will make me die and then give me life again; it is He who, as I ardently desire, will forgive my faults on Judgment day" (XXVI 78-82).

The moment Nimrod wanted to throw Abraham into the fire, the Angel Gabriel asked him, "Do you want anything?"

Abraham, confident in God, replied, "Nothing that comes from you."

—Lahiji

UNITE THE TWO

Whoever has the outer law without the inner reality
Has abandoned the True Way.
Whoever has the inner reality without the outer law
Is nothing but a heretic.
Unite the two, and you will be realized.

—Traditional Sufi saying

152

THE DEGREE BEYOND WHICH
NO OTHER STATION EXISTS

Obaydah never bothered her guide, Malek Dinar, with any questions, except on one occasion when she asked, "When does the devotee attain a degree above all other stations?" Malek replied, "When a devotee reaches a degree beyond which no other station exists, he will not love anything without arriving at God all the sooner!"

Obaydah wept on so hearing this that she fainted and fell.

—Attar

WATCH AND SEE

If you see someone who has been graced with such divine favors that he can fly up into the air, do not be deceived. Watch and see how you find him with the command and prohibition, the guarding of boundaries, and the carrying out of the Law.

—Bayazid Bistami

THE PERFECT MAN

The Perfect Man is one who, in all perfection,
Acts like a slave despite his Lordship.
Then, when he has come to the end of his journey,
Reality places on his head the Crown of Ruler.
He finds eternal life after dying to himself
And begins a fresh path from his End to his Origin.
Clothing himself in the Law like an exterior cloak,
He makes of the Mystic Way his inmost being.
Know that the Truth is the degree of his nature —
He comprehends at once belief and unbelief.
He is adorned with all dazzling virtues, and praised
For his consciousness, his devotion, his holy calm.
All things are in him, but he is far from everything,
Sheltered under the dais of the veils of Mystery.

—Shabistari

WHEN THE DAY CAME

When the Day came —
The Day I had lived and died for —
The Day that is not in any calendar —
Clouds heavy with love
Showered me with wild abundance.
Inside me, my soul was drenched.
Around me, even the desert grew green.

—Kabir

THE DROP AND THE SEA

I went looking for Him
And lost myself;
The drop merged with the Sea —
Who can find it now?

Looking and looking for Him
I lost myself;
The Sea merged with the drop —
Who can find it now?

—Kabir

155

THAT NOTHING

One day, a King entered his royal court and saw that there was a stranger present who, unlike all the others, did not bow to him. He was shaken by such insolence and called out, "How dare you not bow down before me! Only God does not bow down before me, and there is nothing greater than God! Who then are you?"

The ragged stranger answered with a smile, "I am that nothing."

—Traditional Sufi story

LOVE IS HERE

Love is here; it is the blood in my veins, my skin.
I am destroyed; He has filled me with Passion.
His fire has flooded the nerves of my body.
Who am I? Just my name; the rest is Him.

—Rumi

No One Here but Him

Watching my hand; He is moving it.
Hearing my voice; He is speaking. . . .
Walking from room to room —
No one here but Him.

—Rumi

My Body Is Flooded

My body is flooded
With the flame of Love.
My soul lives in
A furnace of bliss.

Love's fragrance
Fills my mouth,
And fans through all things
With each outbreath.

—Kabir

STANDING OF GLORY

No one possesses Glory but Me;
To no one is Glory appropriate but Me;
I am the Glorious One,
Whose nearness cannot be endured,
Whose brilliance no one can stand to be prolonged.

I manifested All That Is,
And am more manifest than It.
Its nearness does not attain to Me;
Its existence is not guided to me.

I hide the Inward of the Inward,
And am more hidden than It.
No sign of it applies to Me,
No path of it leads truly to Me.

I am nearer to each thing
Than its gnosis of itself;
Its gnosis of itself does not pass
Beyond itself to Me,
And it does not know itself
So long as itself
Is the object of its gnosis.

Without Me, how could the eyes see what is proper to them?
Without Me, how could the ears have heard what is theirs to hear?

If I had ever spoken the Word of Glory,
It would have scythed down all perception,

It would have annihilated all gnosis like the desert
On the day the wind sweeps over it.

If the voice of Glory had spoken,
The voices of every qualification
Would have gone dumb forever,
The attainments of every attribute
Would have reeled back to Nothingness.

Where is the one that makes My gnosis
A way of coming to Me?
If I had shown him the Tongue of Sovereignty
His gnosis would have staggered back into ignorance
And he would have been shaken
As the heavens are on the Day of Judgment.

Do not complain I did not cause you
To witness my Glory;
In whatever you witness,
I have given you the gift of abasement;
I have hacked you in splendor to your knees.

The party of people of heaven and earth
Are all in abasement and hemmed in by My Glory
But I have servants

Whom heaven cannot contain with all its spheres,
Whose hearts the sides of the universe cannot support.

I have caused the eyes of their hearts
To witness the Lights of My Glory
Which only fall on anything
To annihilate it.

Their hearts see nothing in the nine heavens
They could affirm
And they have nowhere to return to on earth,
Nowhere they can live.

Take whatever you need
To concentrate yourself on Me,
Or I will fling you back into need
And separate you from Me.

When My Gnosis is present
No need can exist;
While My Gnosis is arriving
Take whatever you need.

— Niffari

IN THE SEVENTH HEAVEN

I continued to fly and wander through kingdom after kingdom, veil after veil, realm after realm, sea after sea, curtain after curtain, until I finally came to a throne. I was received there by angels. Their eyes were as innumerable as the stars of heaven. From each eye flamed a light that illumined the one who gazed at it. Those lights became lamps. From inside the lamps I heard chants of praise and divine unity.

I continued to fly like that until I came to a sea of light with crashing waves. Beside that light, the sun is dark. On the sea there was a ship of light. Beside its light, the light of the seas themselves were dark.

I continued to cross sea after sea until I came to the greatest sea on which stood the Royal Throne of the Compassionate One. I went on singing His praises until I saw that all there was — from the throne to the earth, from cherubim to angels, to the bearers of the royal throne to others created by Allah the Glorious in all the heavens and the earth — was smaller from the view of the flight of the secret of my heart in search of Him, than a mustard seed between sky and earth.

He continued to show me some of the miraculous subtleties of His generosity, and the majestic fullness of His power, and the great vastness of His sovereignty which it would wear out the tongue to attempt to describe. Through all these marvels I kept saying, "O my Beloved, my true goal is different from everything you are showing me. . . ."

And when Allah the Glorious knew the sincerity of my will in looking for Him and Him alone, He cried out, "To Me! To Me!" and then said, "O my chosen one, come near to Me and gaze on the plains of my Splendor and all the realms of my Radiance. Sit upon the carpet of my Holiness until you see the subtleties of my I-ness as It endlessly crafts the universes. You are my chosen one, my beloved, and the finest of all my creatures."

When I heard that, it was as if I were melting like melting lead. Then He gave me a drink from the spring of Graciousness with the cup of Intimacy. Then He brought me closer and closer to Him until I was nearer to Him than the spirit is to the body.

—Bayazid Bistami

HOW KING TUKLA WAS REBUKED BY A HOLY MAN

Tukla, King of Persia, once visited a holy man and said, "My years on the earth have been useless. Only a holy beggar man like you carries away riches from this world to the next. All I want to do now is to sit in the corner of devotion and spend the rest of my days in prayer."

"Nonsense!" the holy man cried. "Religion consists in the service of the people; you do not need accessories like a rosary, or prayer rug, or tattered robe. Be a king in power and a devotee in purity of morals. Action, not words, are demanded by true religion; words without action are hollow."

—Sadi

O LORD, GIVE ME EYES

O Lord, give me eyes
That see nothing but Your Glory.
Give me a mind
That finds joy in Your service.
Give me a soul
Drunk on the wine of Your wisdom.

—Sheikh Ansari

TOTAL DEDICATION

O Lord, may my mind reel with revelations of You,
May my heart blaze with the mysteries of Your grace,
May my tongue move only to sing
Your praise.

—Sheikh Ansari

GIVE ME

O Lord, give me a heart
I can pour out in thanksgiving.
Give me life
So I can spend it
Working for the salvation of the world.

—Sheikh Ansari

FINAL PRAYER

O MY GOD, LIGHT OF LIGHTS

O my God, Light of lights and ruler of all the spheres, You are the first, there was none before You; You are the last, there shall be none after You. The angels cannot comprehend Your majesty and human beings cannot reach the knowledge of the perfection of Your Essence.

O God, set us free from the things that chain us, and deliver us from all evil that may hinder us. Send down upon our spirits Your gracious influence and irradiate our souls with the brilliance of Your light. The mind is only a drop in the ocean of Your Kingdom and the soul only a spark of Your Divine Glory.

Praise be to You whom no eyes can see, whose likeness no thought can imagine; to You be thanksgiving and praise. You give and You take away: You are the All-Bountiful and the All-Abiding. Praise be to You always, for Yours is the power over all things and unto You shall we return.

—Suhrawardi Halabi

ACKNOWLEDGMENTS

❖

Our profoundest thanks to:

Leila and Henry Luce III, for all their protecting love.

Gloria Cooper, for the tender nobility of her spirit.

Mollie Corcoran, for her unfailing kindness.

Our editor, Brenda Rosen, for her faith and clarity of heart.

Our designer, Beth Hansen-Winter, for the truth of her taste.

Our copy editor, Dawna Elaine Page, for all her heartfelt and scrupulous work.

William Chittick and Peter Wilson, the distinguished translators of *Divine Flashes* by Fakhruddin Iraqi wrote, "We have tried to 'trans-create' as well as translate, to offer something that will stand on its own as a work in English literature and that will provide a more exact rendition of Iraqi's meaning than a merely literal translation could attain." These principles have been the constant inspiration for *Perfume of the Desert*; I wanted to create a comprehensive Sufi mystical "symphony" in five carefully composed parts, each made up of inspiring texts rendered in as precise, fresh, and lucid a way as possible.

For my "trans-creations" of Rumi, Shabistari, Lahiji, Ibn Arabi, and Sultan Valad, I have relied considerably on the translations into French of their work by the great Islamic scholar,

Eva de Vitray Meyerovitch, with whom I worked in Paris and whose example of both rigor and poetic sensitivity has served as a touchstone for whatever work I have done in this field. My versions of Kabir refer richly to versions by Tagore and V. K. Sethi; those of Rabia rely to some extent on those of Charles Upton in his book *Doorkeeper of the Heart* which first made me aware of the range of Rabia's poetic genius. My work on Sadi has been influenced by a whole group of nineteenth-century and contemporary translators in several European languages, most notably Edward Rehatsek. My trans-creations of Sheikh Ansari owe much to this faithful renderings of Sir Jogendra Singh. A. J. Arberry's translations helped me to create clear versions of Attar Al-Hallaj, Bayazid Bistami, Jami, Muhasibi, and Niffari. Idries Shah's transcreations of Nasrudin helped me in preparing my own. Two books have been especially inspiring to me in my search for material: *Traveling the Path of Love* by Llewellyn Vaughan-Lee (Golden Sufi Center Publishing) and *Early Islamic Mysticism* in the Classics of Western Spirituality Series (Paulist Press); both led me to texts and mystical writers I would not otherwise have known, and I am grateful for their guidance.

I wish there was room here to thank all the fine scholars and translators to whom I owe more than words can express. If I have been able to do anything in *Perfume of the Desert* to bring the glory of the Sufi mystical tradition to others, it is because of their help and inspiration and passion. May the Beloved embrace and bless them all with His Eternal Presence of Love!